SOCIAL REFORM or REVOLUTION?

ROSA
LUXEMBURG

SANAGE
PUBLISHING HOUSE

Paperback: 978-939574170-5

Printed by:

Sanage Publishing House LLP
Mumbai, India

sanagepublishing@gmail.com

Rosa Luxemburg (5 March 1871 – 15 January 1919) was a Polish and naturalised-German revolutionary socialist, Marxist philosopher and anti-war activist. Successively, she was a member of the Proletariat party, the Social Democracy of the Kingdom of Poland and Lithuania (SDKPiL), the Social Democratic Party of Germany (SPD), the Independent Social Democratic Party (USPD), the Spartacus League (Spartakusbund), and the Communist Party of Germany (KPD).

Due to her pointed criticism of both the Leninist and the more moderate social democratic schools of socialism, Luxemburg has had a somewhat ambivalent reception among scholars and theorists of the political left.

Born and raised in an assimilated Jewish family in Poland, she became a German citizen in 1897

CONTENTS

Introduction

At first view the title of this work may be found surprising. Can the Social-Democracy be against reforms? Can we contrapose the social revolution, the transformation of the existing order, our final goal, to social reforms? Certainly not. The daily struggle for reforms, for the amelioration of the condition of the workers within the framework of the existing social order, and for democratic institutions, offers to the Social-Democracy the only means of engaging in the proletarian class war and working in the direction of the final goal, the conquest of political power and the suppression of wage labour. Between social reforms and revolution there exists for the Social Democracy an indissoluble tie. The struggle for reforms is its means, the social revolution, its aim.

It is in Eduard Bernstein's theory, presented in his articles on *Problems of Socialism, Neue Zeit* of 1897–98, and in his book *Die Voraussetzungen des Socialismus und die Aufgaben der Sozialdemokratie*[1] that we find, for the first time, the opposition of the two factors of the labour movement. His theory tends to counsel us to renounce the social trans-formation, the final goal of Social-Democracy and, inversely, to make of social reforms, the means of the class struggle, its aim. Bernstein himself has very clearly and characteristically formulated this viewpoint when he wrote: "The Final goal, no matter what it is, is nothing; the movement is everything."

---

1. *The Pre-Conditions of Socialism and the Tasks for Social Democracy* [English translation: *Evolutionary Socialism]*

But since the final goal of socialism constitutes the only decisive factor distinguishing the Social-Democratic movement from bourgeois democracy and from bourgeois radicalism, the only factor transforming the entire labour movement from a vain effort to repair the capitalist order into a class struggle against this order, for the suppression of this order—the question: "Reform or Revolution?" as it is posed by Bernstein, equals for the Social-Democracy the question: "To be or not to be?" In the controversy with Bernstein and his followers, everybody in the Party ought to understand clearly it is not a question of this or that method of struggle, or the use of this or that set of tactics, but of the very existence of the Social-Democratic movement.

Upon a casual consideration of Bernstein's theory, this may appear like an exaggeration. Does he not continually mention the Social-Democracy and its aims? Does he not repeat again and again, in very explicit language, that he too strives toward the final goal of socialism, but in another way? Does he not stress particularly that he fully approves of the present practice of the Social-Democracy?

That is all true, to be sure. It is also true that every new movement, when it first elaborates its theory and policy, begins by finding support in the preceding movement, though it may be in direct contradiction with the latter. It begins by suiting itself to the forms found at hand and by speaking the language spoken hereto. In time the new grain breaks through the old husk. The new movement finds its forms and its own language.

To expect an opposition against scientific socialism at its very beginning, to express itself clearly, fully and to the last consequence on the subject of its real content: to expect it to deny openly and bluntly the theoretic basis of the Social-Democracy would amount to under-rating the power of scientific socialism. Today he who wants to pass as a socialist, and at the same time declare war on Marxian doctrine, the most stupendous product of the human mind in the century, must begin with involuntary esteem for Marx. He must begin by acknowledging himself to be his disciple, by seeking in Marx's own teachings the points of support for an attack on the latter, while he represents this attack as a further development of Marxian doctrine. On this account, we must, unconcerned by its outer forms, pick out the sheathed kernel of Bernstein's theory. This is a matter of urgent necessity for the broad layers of the industrial proletariat in our Party.

No coarser insult, no baser aspersion, can be thrown against the workers than the remarks: "Theocratic controversies are only for academicians." Some time ago Lassalle said: "Only when science and the workers, these opposite poles of society, become one, will they crush in their arms of steel all obstacles to culture." The entire strength of the modern labour movement rests on theoretic knowledge.

But doubly important is this knowledge for the workers in the present case because it is precisely, they and their influence in the movement that are in the balance here. It is their skin that is being brought to market. The opportunist theory in the Party, the theory formulated by Bernstein, is nothing else than an unconscious attempt to assure predominance to the petty-bourgeois elements that have entered our Party, to change the policy and aims of our Party in their direction. The question of reform or revolution, of the final goal and the movement, is basically, in another form, but the question of the petty-bourgeois or proletarian character of the labour movement.

It is, therefore, in the interest of the proletarian mass of the Party to become acquainted, actively and in detail, with the present theoretic knowledge remains the privilege of a handful of "academicians" in the Party, the latter will face the danger of going astray. Only when the great mass of workers take the keen and dependable weapons of scientific socialism in their own hands, will all the petty-bourgeois inclinations, all the opportunistic currents, come to naught. The movement will then find itself on sure and firm ground. "Quantity will do it"

- - -

CHAPTER I.

The Opportunist Method

If it is true that theories are only the images of the phenomena of the exterior world in the human consciousness, it must be added, concerning Eduard Bernstein's system, that theories are sometimes inverted images. Think of a theory of instituting socialism by means of social reforms in the face of the complete stagnation of the reform movement in Germany. Think of a theory of trade union control. Consider the theory of winning a majority in Parliament, after the revision of the constitution of Saxony and in view of the most recent attempts against universal suffrage. However, the pivotal point of Bernstein's system is not located in his conception of the practical tasks of the Social-Democracy. It is found in his stand on the course of the objective development of capitalist society, which, in turn is closely bound to his conception of the practical tasks of the Social-Democracy.

According to Bernstein, a general decline of capitalism seems to be increasingly improbable because, on the one hand, capitalism shows a greater capacity of adaptation, and, on the other hand, capitalist production becomes more and more varied.

The capacity of capitalism to adapt itself, says Bernstein, is manifested first in the disappearance of general crises, resulting from the development of the credit system, employers' organizations, wider means of communication and informational services. It shows itself secondly, in the tenacity of the middle classes, which hails from the growing differentiation of the branches of production and the elevation of vast layers of the proletariat to the level of the middle class. It is furthermore proved, argues Bernstein, by the amelioration of the economic and political situation of the proletariat as a result of its trade union activity.

From this theoretic stand is derived the following general conclusion about the practical work of the Social-Democracy. The latter must not direct its daily activity toward the conquest of political power but toward the betterment of the condition of the working class, within the existing order. It must not expect to institute socialism as a result of a political and social crisis but should build socialism by means of the progressive extension of social control and the gradual application of the principle of co-operation.

Bernstein himself sees nothing new in his theories. On the contrary, he believes them to be in agreement with certain declarations of Marx and Engels. Nevertheless, it seems to us that it is difficult to deny that they are in formal contradiction with the conceptions of scientific socialism.

If Bernstein's revisionism merely consisted in affirming that the march of capitalist development is slower than was thought before, he would merely be presenting an argument for adjourning the conquest of power by the proletariat, on which everybody agreed up to now. Its only consequence would be a slowing up of the pace of the struggle.

But that is not the case. What Bernstein questions is not the rapidity of the development of capitalist society, but the march of the development itself and, consequently, the very possibility of a change to socialism.

Socialist theory up to now declared that the point of departure for a transformation to socialism would be a general and catastrophic crisis. We must distinguish in this outlook two things: the fundamental idea and its exterior form.

The fundamental idea consists of the affirmation that capitalism, as a result of its own inner contradictions, moves toward a point when it will be unbalanced, when it will simply become impossible. There were good reasons for conceiving that juncture in the form of a catastrophic general commercial crisis. But that is of secondary importance when the fundamental idea is considered.

The scientific basis of socialism rests, as is well known, on three principal results of capitalist development. First, on the growing anarchy of capitalist economy, leading inevitably to its ruin. Second, on the progressive socialization of the process of production, which creates the germs of the future social order. And third, on the increased organization and consciousness of the proletarian class, which constitutes the active factor in the coming revolution.

Bernstein pulls away from the first of the three fundamental supports of scientific socialism. He says that capitalist development does not lead to a general economic collapse.

He does not merely reject a certain form of the collapse. He rejects the very possibility of collapse. He says textually: "One could claim that by collapse of the present society is meant something else than a general commercial crisis, worse than all others, that is a complete collapse of the capitalist system brought about as a result of its own contradictions." And to this he replies: "With the growing development of society a complete and almost general collapse of the present system of production becomes more and more improbable, because capitalist development increases on the one hand the capacity of adaptation and, on the other that is at the same time, the differentiation of industry." (Neue Zeit, 1897-98, Vol.18, p. 555)

But then the question arises: Why and how, in that case, can we attain the final goal? According to scientific socialism, the historic necessity of the socialist revolution manifests itself above all in the growing anarchy of capitalism, which drives the system into an impasse. But if one admits with Bernstein that capitalist development does not move in the direction of its own ruin, then socialism ceases to be objectively necessary. There remain the other two mainstays of the scientific explanation of socialism, which are also said to be consequences of capitalism itself: the socialization of the process of production and the growing consciousness of the proletariat. It is these two matters that Bernstein has in mind when he says: "The suppression of the theory of collapse does not in any way deprive socialist doctrine of the power of persuasion. For, examined closely, what are all factors enumerated by us that make for the suppression or the modification of the former crises? Nothing else, in fact than the conditions, or even in party the germs, of the socialization of production and exchange." (*Ibid.*, p. 554)

Very little reflection is needed to understand that here too we face a false conclusion. Where lies the importance of all the phenomena that are said by Bernstein to be the means of capitalist adaptation cartels, the credit system, the development of means of communication, the amelioration of the situation of the working class, etc.? Obviously, in that they suppress or, at least, attenuate the internal contradictions of capitalist economy, and stop the development or the aggravation of these contradictions. Thus, the suppression of crises can only mean the suppression of the antagonism between production and exchange on the capitalist base. The amelioration of the situation of the working class, or the penetration of certain fractions of the class into middle layers, can only mean the attenuation of the antagonism between Capital and Labour. But if the mention factors suppress the capitalist contradictions and consequently save the system from ruin, if they enable capitalism to maintain itself and that is why Bernstein calls them "means of adaptation", how can cartels, the credit system, trade unions, etc., be at the same time "the conditions and even, in part, the germs" of socialism? Obviously only in the sense that they express most clearly the social character of production.

But by presenting it in its capitalist form, the same factors render superfluous, inversely, in the same measure, the transformation of this socialized production into socialist production. That is why they can be the germs or conditions of a socialist order only in a theoretic sense and not in an historic sense. They are phenomena which, in the light of our conception of socialism, we know to be related to socialism but which, in fact, not only do not lead to a socialist revolution but render it, on the contrary, superfluous.

There remains one force making for socialism, the class consciousness of the proletariat. But it, too, is in the given case no the simple intellectual reflection of the growing contradictions of capitalism and its approaching decline. It is now no more than an ideal whose force of persuasion rests only on the perfection attributed to it.

We have here, in brief, the explanation of the socialist programme by means of "pure reason." We have here, to use simpler language, an idealist explanation of socialism. The objective necessity of socialism, the explanation of socialism as the result of the material development of society, falls to the ground.

Revisionist theory thus places itself in a dilemma. Either the socialist transformation is, as was admitted up to now, the consequence of the internal contradictions of capitalism, and with the growth of capitalism will develop its inner contradictions, resulting inevitably, at some point, in its collapse, (in that case the "means of adaptation" are ineffective and the theory of collapse is correct); or the "means of adaptation" will really stop the collapse of the capitalist system and thereby enable capitalism to maintain itself by suppressing its own contradictions. In that case socialism ceases to be an historic necessity. It then becomes anything you want to call it, but it is no longer the result of the material development of society.

The dilemma leads to another. Either revisionism is correct in its position on the course of capitalist development, and therefore the socialist transformation of society is only a utopia, or socialism is not a utopia, and the theory of "means of adaptation" is false. There is the question in a nutshell.

– – –

CHAPTER II.

The Adaptation Of Capital

According to Bernstein, the credit system, the perfected means of communication and the new capitalist combines are the important factors that forward the adaptation of capitalist economy.

Credit has diverse applications in capitalism. Its two most import-ant functions are to extend production and to facilitate exchange. When the inner tendency of capitalist production to extend boundlessly strikes against the restricted dimensions of private property, credit appears as a means of surmounting these limits in a particular capitalist manner. Credit, through shareholding, combines in one magnitude of capital a large number of individual capitals. It makes available to each capitalist the use of other capitalists' money in the form of industrial credit. As commercial credit it accelerates the exchange of commodities and therefore the return of capital into production, and thus aids the entire cycle of the process of production. The manner in which these two principal functions of credit influence the formation of crises is quite obvious. If it is true that crises appear as a result of the contradiction existing between the capacity of extension, the tendency of production to increase, and the restricted consumption capacity of the market, credit is precisely, in view of what was stated above, the specific means that makes this contradiction break out as often as possible. To begin with, it increases disproportionately the capacity of the extension of production and thus constitutes an inner motive force that is constantly pushing production to exceed the limits of the market. But credit strikes from two sides. After having (as a factor of the process of production) provoked overproduction, credit (as a factor of exchange) destroys, during the crisis, the very productive forces it itself created. At the first symptom of the crisis, credit melts away. It abandons exchange where it would still be found indispensable, and appearing instead, ineffective, and useless, there were some exchanges still continues, it reduces to a minimum the consumption capacity of the market.

Besides having these two principal results, credit also influences the formation of crises in the following ways. It constitutes the technical means of making available to an entrepreneur the capital of other owners. It stimulates at the same time the bold and unscrupulous utilization of the property of others. That is, it leads to speculation. Credit not only aggravates the crisis in its capacity as a dissembled means of exchange it also helps to bring and extend the crisis by transforming all exchange into an extremely complex and artificial mechanism that, having a minimum of metallic money as a real base, is easily disarranged at the slightest occasion.

We see that credit, instead of being an instrument for the suppression or the attenuation of crises, is on the contrary a particularly mighty instrument for the formation of crises. It cannot be anything else. Credit eliminates the remaining rigidity of capitalist relationships. It introduces everywhere the greatest elasticity possible. It renders all capitalist forces extensible, relative, and mutually sensitive to the highest degree. Doing this, it facilitates and aggravates crises, which are nothing more or less than the periodic collisions of the contradictory forces of capitalist economy.

That leads us to another question. Why does credit generally have the appearance of a "means of adaptation" of capitalism? No matter what the relation or form in which this "adaptation" is represented by certain people, it can obviously consist only of the power to suppress one of the several antagonistic relations of capitalist economy, that is, of the power to suppress or weaken one of these contradictions, and allow liberty of movement, at one point or another, to the other fettered productive forces. In fact, it is precisely credit that aggravates these contradictions to the highest degree. It aggravates the antagonism between the mode of production and the mode of exchange by stretching production to the limit and at the same time paralyzing exchange at the smallest pretext. It aggravates the antagonism between the mode of production and the mode of appropriation by separating production from ownership, that is, by transforming the capital employed in production into "social" capital and at the same time transforming a part of the profit, in the form of interest on capital, into a simple title of ownership. It aggravates the antagonism existing between the property relations (ownership) and the relations of production by putting into a small number of hands immense productive forces and expropriating large numbers of small capitalists. Lastly, it aggravates the antagonism existing between social character of production and private capitalist ownership by rendering necessary the intervention of the State in production.

In short, credit reproduces all the fundamental antagonisms of the capitalist world. It accentuates them. It precipitates their development and thus pushes the capitalist world forward to its own destruction. The prime act of capitalist adaptation, as far as credit is concerned, should really consist in breaking and suppressing credit. In fact, credit is far from being a means of capitalist adaptation. It is, on the contrary, a means of destruction of the most extreme revolutionary significance. Has not this revolutionary character of credit actually inspired plans of "socialist" reform? As such, it has had some distinguished proponents, some of whom (Isaac Pereira in France), were, as Marx put it, half profits, half rogues.

Just as fragile is the second "means of adaptation": employers' organizations. According to Bernstein, such organizations will put an end to anarchy of production and do away with crises through their regulation of production. The multiple repercussions of the development of cartels and trusts have not been considered too carefully up to now. But they predict a problem that can only be solved with the aid of Marxist theory.

One thing is certain. We could speak of a damming up of capitalist anarchy through the agency of capitalist combines only in the measure that cartels, trusts, etc., become, even approximately, the dominant form of production. But such a possibility is excluded by the very nature of cartels. The final economic aim and result of combines is the following. Through the suppression of competition in a given branch of production, the distribution of the mass of profit realized on the market is influenced in such a manner that there is an increase of the share going to this branch of industry. Such organization of the field can increase the rate of profit in one branch of industry at the expense of another. That is precisely why it cannot be generalized, for when it is extended to all important branches of industry, this tendency suppresses its own influence.

Furthermore, within the limits of their practical application the result of combines is the very opposite of suppression of industrial anarchy. Cartels ordinarily succeed in obtaining an increase of profit, in the home market, by producing at a lower rate of profit for the foreign market, thus utilizing the supplementary portions of capital which they cannot utilize for domestic needs. That is to say, they sell abroad cheaper than at home. The result is the sharpening of competition abroad, the very opposite of what certain people want to find. That is well demonstrated by the history of the world sugar industry.

Generally speaking, combines treated as a manifestation of the capitalist mode of production, can only be considered a definite phase of capitalist development. Cartels are fundamentally nothing else than a means resorted to by the capitalist mode of production for the purpose of holding back the fatal fall of the rate of profit in certain branches of production. What method do cartels employ for this end? That of keeping inactive a part of the accumulated capital. That is, they use the same method which in another form is employed in crises. The remedy and the illness resemble each other like two drops of water. Indeed, the first can be considered the lesser evil only up to a certain point. When the outlets of disposal begin to shrink, and the world market has been extended to its limit and has become exhausted through the competition of the capitalist countries and sooner or later that is bound to come, then the forced partial idleness of capital will reach such dimensions that the remedy will become transformed into a malady, and capital, already pretty much "Socialized" through regulation, will tend to revert again to the form of individual capital. In the face of the increased difficulties of finding markets, each individual portion of capital will prefer to take its chances alone. At that time, the large regulating organizations will burst like soap bubbles and give way to aggravated competition.

In a general way, cartels, just like credit, appear therefore as a determined phase of capitalist development, which in the last analysis aggravates the anarchy of the capitalist world and expresses and ripens its internal contradictions. Cartels aggravate the antagonism existing between the mode of production and exchange by sharpening the struggle between the producer and consumer, as is the case especially in the United States. They aggravate, furthermore, the antagonism existing between the mode of production and the mode of appropriation by opposing, in the most brutal fashion, to the working class the superior force of organized capital, and thus increasing the antagonism between Capital and Labour.

Finally, capitalist combinations aggravate the contradiction existing between the international character of capitalist world economy and the national character of the State insofar as they are always accompanied by a general tariff war, which sharpens the differences among the capitalist States. We must add to this the decidedly revolutionary influence exercised by cartels on the concentration of production, technical progress, etc.

In other words, when evaluated from the angle of their final effect on capitalist economy, cartels and trusts fail as "means of adaptation."

They fail to attenuate the contradictions of capitalism. On the contrary, they appear to be an instrument of greater anarchy. They encourage the further development of the internal contradictions of capitalism. They accelerate the coming of a general decline of capitalism.

But if the credit system, cartels, and the rest do not suppress the anarchy of capitalism, why have we not had a major commercial crisis for two decades, since 1873? Is this not a sign that, contrary to Marx's analysis the capitalist mode of production has adapted itself at least, in a general way to the needs of society? Hardly had Bernstein rejected, in 1898, Marx's theory of crises, when a profound general crisis broke out in 1900, while seven years later, a new crisis beginning in the United States, hit the world market. Facts proved the theory of "adaptation" to be false. They showed at the same time that the people who abandoned Marx's theory of crisis only because no crisis occurred within a certain space of time merely confused the essence of this theory with one of its secondary exterior aspects the ten-year cycle. The description of the cycle of modern capitalist industry as a ten-year period was to Marx and Engels, in 1860 and 1870, only a simple statement of facts. It was not based on a natural law but on a series of given historic circumstances that were connected with the rapidly spreading activity of young capitalism.

The crisis of 1825 was in effect, the result of extensive investment of capital in the construction of roads, canals, gas works, which took place during the preceding decade, particularly in England, where the crisis broke out. The following crisis of 1836-1839 was similarly the result of heavy investments in the construction of means of transportation. The crisis of 1847 was provoked by the feverish building of railroads in England (from 1844 to 1847, in three years, the British Parliament gave railway concessions to the value of 15 billion dollars). In each of the three mentioned cases, a crisis came after new bases for capitalist development were established. In 1857, the same result was brought by the abrupt opening of new markets for European industry in America and Australia, after the discovery of the gold mines, and the extensive construction of railway lines, especially in France, where the example of England was then closely imitated. (From 1852 to 1856, new railway lines to the value of 1,250 million francs were built in France alone). And finally, we have the great crisis of 1873, a direct consequence of the firm boom of large industry in Germany and Austria, which followed the political events of 1866 and 1871.

So that up to now, the sudden extension of the domain of capitalist economy, and not its shrinking, was each time the cause of the commercial crisis. That the international crisis repeated themselves precisely every ten years was a purely exterior fact, a matter of chance. The Marxist formula for crises as presented by Engels in Anti-Dühring and by Marx in the first and third volumes of Capital, applies to all crises only in the measure that it uncovers their international mechanism and their general basic causes.

Crises may repeat themselves every five or ten years, or even every eight or twenty years. But what proves best the falseness of Bernstein's theory is that it is in the countries having the greatest development of the famous "means of adaptation" credit, perfected communications, and trusts that the last crisis (1907-1908) was most violent.

The belief that capitalist production could "adapt" itself to exchange presupposes one of two things: either the world market can spread unlimitedly, or on the contrary the development of the productive forces is so fettered that it cannot pass beyond the bounds of the market. The first hypothesis constitutes a material impossibility. The second is rendered just as impossible by the constant technical progress that daily creates new productive forces in all branches.

There remains still another phenomenon which, says Bernstein, contradicts the course of capitalist development as it is indicated above. In the "steadfast phalanx" of middle-size enterprises, Bernstein sees a sign that the development of large industry does not move in a revolutionary direction and is not as effective from the angle of the concentration of industry as was expected by the "theory" of collapse. He is here, however, the victim of his own lack of understanding.

For to see the progressive disappearance of large industry is to misunderstand sadly the nature of this process.

According to Marxist theory, small capitalists play in the general course of capitalist development the role of pioneers of technical change. They possess that role in a double sense. They initiate new methods of production in well-established branches of industry; they are instrumental in the creation of new branches of production not yet exploited by the big capitalist. It is false to imagine that the history of the middle-size capitalist establishments proceeds rectilinearly in the direction of their progressive disappearance. The course of this development is on the contrary purely dialectical and moves constantly among contradictions. The middle capitalist layers find themselves, just like the workers, under the influence of two antagonistic tendencies, one ascendant, the other descendant. In this case, the descendent tendency is the continued rise of the scale of production, which overflows periodically the dimensions of the average size parcels of capital and removes them repeatedly from the terrain of world competition.

The ascendant tendency is, first, the periodic depreciation of the existing capital, which lowers again, for a certain time, the scale of production in proportion to the value of the necessary minimum amount of capital. It is represented, besides, by the penetration of capitalist production into new spheres. The struggle of the average size enterprise against big Capital cannot be considered a regularly proceeding battle in which the troops of the weaker party continue to melt away directly and quantitatively. It should be rather regarded as a periodic mowing down of the small enterprises, which rapidly grow up again, only to be mowed down once more by large industry. The two tendencies play ball with the middle capitalist layers. The descending tendency must win in the end.

The very opposite is true about the development of the working class. The victory of the descending tendency must not necessarily show itself in an absolute numerical diminution of the middle-size enterprises.

It must show itself, first in the progressive increase of the minimum amount of capital necessary for the functioning of the enterprises in the old branches of production; second in the constant diminution of the interval of time during which the small capitalists conserve the opportunity to exploit the new branches of production. The result as far as the small capitalist is concerned, is a progressively shorter duration of his stay in the new industry and a progressively more rapid change in the methods of production as a field for investment. For the average capitalist strata, taken as a whole, there is a process of more and more rapid social assimilation and dissimilation.

Bernstein knows this perfectly well. He himself comments on this. But what he seems to forget is that this very thing is the law of the movement of the average capitalist enterprise. If one admits that small capitalists are pioneers of technical progress, and if it true that the latter is the vital pulse of the capitalist economy, then it is manifest that small capitalists are an integral part of capitalist development, which can only disappear together with it [capitalist development]. The progressive disappearance of the middle-size enterprise in the absolute sense considered by Bernstein means not, as he thinks, the revolutionary course of capitalist development, but precisely the contrary, the cessation, the slowing up of development. "The rate of profit, that is to say, the relative increase of capital," said Marx, "is important first of all for new investors of capital, grouping themselves independently. And as soon as the formation of capital falls exclusively into a handful of big capitalists, the revivifying fire of production is extinguished. It dies away."

- - -

CHAPTER III.

The Realization Of Socialism Through Social Reforms

Bernstein rejects the "Theory of Collapse" as an historic road toward socialism. Now what is the way to a socialist society that is pro-posed by his "theory of adaptation to capitalism?" Bernstein answers this question only by allusion. Konrad Schmidt, however, attempts to deal with this detail in the manner of Bernstein. According to him, "the trade union struggle for hours and wages and the political struggle for reforms will lead to a progressively more extensive control over the conditions of production," and "as the rights of the capitalist proprietor will be diminished through legislation, he will be reduced in time to the role of a simple administrator." "The capitalist will see his property lose more and more value to himself" till finally "the direction and administration of exploitation will be taken from him entirely" and "collective exploitation" instituted.

Therefore, trade unions, social reforms and, adds Bernstein, the political democratization of the State are the means of the progressive realization of socialism.

But the fact is that the principal function of trade unions (and this was best explained by Bernstein himself in Neue Zeit in 1891) con-sists in providing the workers with a means of realizing the capitalist law of wages, that is to say, the sale of their labour power at current market prices. Trade unions enable the proletariat to utilize at each instant, the conjuncture of the market. But these conjunctures

(1) The Labour demand determined by the state of production,

(2) The Labour supply created by the proletarianization of the middle strata of society and the natural reproduction of the working classes and

(3) The momentary degree of productivity of labour, these remain outside of the sphere of influence of the trade unions. Trade unions cannot suppress the law of wages. Under the most favourable circumstances, the best they can do is to impose on capitalist exploitation the "normal" limit of the moment. They have not, however, the power to suppress exploitation itself, not even gradually.

Schmidt, it is true, sees the present trade union movement in a "feeble initial stage." He hopes that "in the future" the "trade union movement will exercise a progressively increased influence over the regulation of production." But by the regulation of Production, we can only understand two things: intervention in the technical domain of the process of production and fixing the scale of production itself. What is the nature of the influence exercised by trade unions in these two departments? It is clear that in the technique of production, the interest of the capitalist agrees, up to a certain point, with the progress and development of capitalist economy. It is his own interest that pushes him to make technical improvements. But the isolated worker finds himself in a decidedly different position. Each technical transformation contradicts his interests. It aggravates his helpless situation by depreciating the value of his labour power and rendering his work more intense, more monotonous, and more difficult.

Insofar as trade unions can intervene in the technical department of production, they can only oppose technical innovation. But here they do not act in the interest of the entire working class and its emancipation, which accords rather with technical progress and, therefore, with the interest of the isolated capitalist. They act here in a reactionary direction. And in fact, we find efforts on the part of workers to intervene in the technical part of production not in the future, where Schmidt looks for it, but in the past of the trade union movement. Such efforts characterized the old phase of English trade unionism (up to 1860), when the British organizations were still tied to medieval "corporative" vestiges and found inspiration in the outworn principle of "a fair day's wage for a fair day's labour," as expressed by Webb in his History of Trade Unionism.

On the other hand, the effort of the labour unions to fix the scale of production and the prices of commodities is a recent phenomenon. Only recently have we witnessed such attempts and again in England.

In their nature and tendencies, these efforts resemble those dealt with above. What does the active participation of trade unions in fixing the scale and cost of production amount to? It amounts to a cartel of the workers and entrepreneurs in a common stand against the consumer and especially rival entrepreneurs. In no way is the effect of this any different from that of ordinary employers' associations. Basically, we no longer have here a struggle between Labour and Capital, but the solidarity of Capital and Labour against the total consumers. Considered for its social worth, it is seen to be a reactionary move that cannot be a stage in the struggle for the emancipation of the proletariat, because it connotes the very opposite of the class struggle. Considered from the angle of practical application, it is found to be a utopia which, as shown by a rapid examination, cannot be extended to the large branches of industry producing for the world market.

So that the scope of trade unions is limited essentially to a struggle for an increase of wages and the reduction of labour time, that is to say, to efforts at regulating capitalist exploitation as they are made necessary by the momentary situation of the old-world market. But labour unions can in no way influence the process of production itself. Moreover, trade union development moves contrary to what is asserted by Konrad Schmidt in the direction of a complete detachment of the labour market from any immediate relation to the rest of the market.

That is shown by the fact that even attempts to relate labour contracts to the general situation of production by means of a system of sliding wage scales have been outmoded with historic development. The British labour unions are moving farther and farther away from such efforts.

Even within the effective boundaries of its activity the trade union movement cannot spread in the unlimited way claimed for it by the theory of adaptation. On the contrary, if we examine the large factors of social development, we see that we are not moving toward an epoch marked by a victorious development of trade unions, but rather toward a time when the hardships of labour unions will increase. Once industrial development has attained its highest possible point and capitalism has entered its descending phase on the world market, the trade union struggle will become doubly difficult. In the first place, the objective conjuncture of the market will be less favourable to the sellers of labour power, because the demand for labour power will increase at a slower rate and labour supply more rapidly than at present. In the second place, the capitalists themselves, in order to make up for losses suffered on the world market, will make even greater efforts than at present to reduce the part of the total product going to the workers (in the form of wages). The reduction of wages is, as pointed out by Marx, one of the principal means of retarding the fall of profit. The situation in England already offers us a picture of the beginning of the second stage of trade union development. Trade union action is reduced of necessity to the simple defense of already realized gains, and even that is becoming more and more difficult. Such is the general trend of things in our society. The counterpart of this tendency should be the development of the political side of the class struggle.

Konrad Schmidt commits the same error of historic perspective when he deals with social reforms. He expects that social reforms, like trade union organizations, will "dictate to the capitalists the only conditions under which they will be able to employ labour power." Seeing reform in this light, Bernstein calls labour legislation a piece of "social control," and as such, a piece of socialism. Similarly, Konrad Schmidt always uses the term "social control" when he refers to labour protection laws. Once he has thus happily transformed the State into society, he confidently adds: "That is to say, the rising working class." As a result of this trick of substitution, the innocent labour laws enacted by the German Federal Council are transformed into transitory socialist measures supposedly enacted by the German proletariat.

The mystification is obvious. We know that the present State is not "society" representing the "rising working class." It is itself the representative of capitalist society. It is a class state. Therefore, its reform measures are not an application of "social control," that is, the control of society working freely in its own labour process. They are forms of control applied by the class organization of Capital to the production of Capital. The so-called social reforms are enacted in the interests of Capital. Yes, Bernstein and Konrad Schmidt see at present only "feeble beginnings" of this control. They hope to see a long succession of reforms in the future, all favouring the working class. But here they commit a mistake similar to their belief in the unlimited development of the trade union movement.

A basic condition for the theory of the gradual realization of socialism through social reforms is a certain objective development of capitalist property and of the State. Konrad Schmidt says that the capitalist proprietor tends to lose his special rights with historic development and is reduced to the role of a simple administrator. He thinks that the expropriation of the means of production cannot possibly be affected as a single historic act. He therefore resorts to the theory of expropriation by stages. With this in mind, he divides the right to property into

(1) the right of "sovereignty" (ownership), which he attributes to a thing called "society" and which he wants to extend and

(2) its opposite, the simple right of use, held by the capitalist, but which is supposedly being reduced in the hands of the capitalists to the mere administration of their enterprises.

This interpretation is either a simple play on words, and in that case the theory of gradual expropriation has no real basis, or it is a true picture of judicial development, in which case, as we shall see, the theory of gradual expropriation is entirely false.

The division of the right of property into several component rights, an arrangement serving Konrad Schmidt as a shelter wherein he may construct his theory of "expropriation by stages," characterized feudal society, founded on natural economy. In feudalism, the total product was shared among the social classes of the time on the basis of the personal relations existing between the feudal lord and his serfs or ten-ants. The decomposition of property into several partial rights reflected the manner of distribution of the social wealth of that period. With the passage to the production of commodities and the dissolution of all personal bonds among the participants in the process of production, the relation between men and things (that is to say, private property) became reciprocally stronger. Since the division is no longer made on the basis of personal relations but through exchange, the different rights to a share in the social wealth are no longer measured as fragments of property rights having a common interest. They are measured according to the values brought by each on the market.

The first change introduced into juridical relations with the advance of commodity production in the medieval city communes, was the development of absolute private property. The latter appeared in the very midst of the feudal juridical relations. This development has progressed at a rapid pace in capitalist production. The more the process of production is socialized, the more the process of distribution (division of wealth) rests on exchange. And the more private property becomes inviolable and closed, the more capitalist property becomes transformed from the right to the product of one's own labour to the simple right to appropriate somebody else's labour. As long as the capitalist himself manages his own factory, distribution is still, up to a certain point, tied to his personal participation in the process of production. But as the personal management on the part of the capitalist becomes superfluous, which is the case in the share-holding societies today, the property of capital, so far as its right to share in the distribution (division of wealth) is concerned, becomes separated from any personal relation with production. It now appears in its purest form. The capitalist right to property reaches its most complete development in capital held in the shape of shares and industrial credit.

So that Konrad Schmidt's historic schema, tracing the transformation of the capitalist "from a proprietor to a simple administrator," belies the real historic development. In historic reality, on the contrary, the capitalist tends to change from a proprietor and administrator to a simple proprietor. What happens here to Konrad Schmidt, happened to Goethe:

> *What is, he sees as in a dream.*
> *What no longer is, becomes for him reality.*

Just as Schmidt's historic schema travels, economically, backwards from a modern share-holding society to an artisan's shop, so, juridically, he wishes to lead back the capitalist world into the old feudal shell of the Middle Ages.

Also, from this point of view, "social control" appears in reality under a different aspect than seen by Konrad Schmidt. What functions today as "social control" labour legislation, the control of industrial organizations through shareholding, etc. has absolutely nothing to do with his "supreme ownership." Far from being, as Schmidt believes, a reduction of capitalist ownership, his "social control," is, on the contrary, a protection of such ownership. Or, expressed from the economic viewpoint, it is not a threat to capitalist exploitation, but simply the regulation of exploitation. When Bernstein asks if there is more or less of socialism in a labour protective law, we can assure him that, in the best of labour protective laws, there is no more "socialism" than in a municipal ordinance regulating the cleaning of streets or the lighting of streetlamps.

– – –

CHAPTER IV.

Capitalism And The State

The second condition of the gradual realization of socialism is according to Bernstein, the evolution of the State in society. It has become a commonplace to say that the present State is a class State. This, too, like referring to capitalist society, should not be understood in a rigorous absolute manner, but dialectically.

The State became capitalist with the political victory of the bourgeoisie. Capitalist development modifies essentially the nature of the State, widening its sphere of action, constantly imposing on its new functions (especially those affecting economic life), making more and more necessary its intervention and control in society. In this sense, capitalist development prepares little by little the future fusion of the State to society. It prepares, so to say, the return of the function of the state to society. Following this line of thought, one can speak of an evolution of the capitalist State into society, and it is undoubtedly what Marx had in mind when he referred to labour legislation as the first conscious intervention of "society" in the vital social process, a phrase upon which Bernstein leans heavily.

But on the other hand, the same capitalist development realizes another transformation in the nature of the State. The present State is, first of all, an organization of the ruling class. It assumes functions favouring social developments specifically because, and in the measure that, these interests and social developments coincide, in a general fashion, with the interests of the dominant class. Labour legislation is enacted as much in the immediate interest of the capitalist class as in the interest of society in general. But this harmony endures only up to a certain point of capitalist development. When capitalist development has reached a certain level, the interests of the bourgeoisie, as a class, and the needs of economic progress begin to clash even in the capitalist sense. We believe that this phase has already begun. It shows itself in two extremely important phenomena of contemporary social life on the one hand, the policy of tariff barriers, and on the other, militarism. These two phenomena have played an indispensable, and in that sense a progressive and revolutionary role in the history of capitalism. Without tariff protection the development of large industry would have been impossible in several countries. But now the situation is different.

At present, protection does not serve so much to develop young industry as to maintain artificially certain aged forms of production.

From the angle of capitalist development, that is, from the point of view of world economy, it matters little whether Germany exports more merchandise into England or England exports more merchandise into Germany. From the viewpoint of this development, it may be said that the blackamoor has done his work and it is time for him to go his way. Given the condition of reciprocal dependence in which the various branches of industry find themselves, a protectionist tariff on any commodity necessarily results in raising the cost of production of other commodities inside the country. It therefore impedes industrial development. But this is not so from the viewpoint of the interests of the capitalist class. While industry does not need tariff barriers for its development, the entrepreneurs need tariffs to protect their markets. This signifies that at present tariffs no longer serve as a means of protecting a developing capitalist section against a more advanced section. They are now the arm used by one national group of capitalists against another group. Furthermore, tariffs are no longer necessary as an instrument of protection for industry in its movement to create and conquer the home market. They are now indispensable means for the cartelization of industry, that is, means used in the struggle of capitalist producers against consuming society in the aggregate. What brings out in an emphatic manner the specific character of contemporary customs policies is the fact that today not industry, but agriculture plays the predominant role in the making of tariffs. The policy of customs protection has become a tool for converting and expressing the feudal interests in capitalist form.

The same change has taken place in militarism. If we consider history as it was not as it could have been or should have been, we must agree that war has been an indispensable feature of capitalist development. The United States, Germany, Italy, the Balkan States, Poland, all owe the condition or the rise of their capitalist development to wars, whether resulting in victory or defeat. As long as there were countries marked by internal political division or economic isolation which had to be destroyed, militarism played a revolutionary role, considered from the viewpoint of capitalism. But at present the situation is different. If world politics have become the stage of menacing conflicts, it is not so much a question of the opening of new countries to capitalism. It is a question of already existing European antagonisms, which, transported into other lands, have exploded there. The armed opponents we see today in Europe and on other continents do not range themselves as capitalist countries on one side and backward countries on the other. They are States pushed to war especially as a result of their similarly advanced capitalist development. In view of this, an explosion is certain to be fatal to this development, in the sense that it must provoke an extremely profound disturbance and transformation of economic life in all countries.

However, the matter appears entirely different when considered from the standpoint of the capitalist class. For the latter militarism has become indispensable. First, as a means of struggle for the defense of "national" interests in competition against other "national" groups. Second, as a method of placement for financial and industrial capital. Third, as an instrument of class domination over the labouring population inside the country. In themselves, these interests have nothing in common with the development of the capitalist mode of production. What demonstrates best the specific character of present-day militarism is the fact that it develops generally in all countries as an effect, so to speak, of its own internal, mechanical, motive power, a phenomenon that was completely unknown several decades ago. We recognize this in the fatal character of the impending explosion which is inevitable in spite of the complete impending explosion which is inevitable in spite of the complete indecisiveness of the objectives and motives of the conflict. From a motor of capitalist development militarism has changed into a capitalist malady.

In the clash between capitalist development and the interest of the dominant class, the State takes a position alongside of the latter. Its policy, like that of the bourgeoisie, comes into conflict with social development. It thus loses more and more of its character as a representative of the whole of society and is transformed, at the same rate into a pure class state. Or, to speak more exactly, these two qualities distinguish themselves more from each other and find themselves in a contradictory relation in the very nature of the State. This contradiction becomes progressively sharper. For on one hand, we have the growth of the functions of a general interest on the part of the State, its intervention in social life, its "control" over society. But on the other hand, its class character obliges the State to move the pivot of its activity and its means of coercion more and more into domains which are useful only to the class character of the bourgeoisie and have for society as a whole only a negative importance, as in the case of militarism and tariff and colonial policies. Moreover, the "social control" exercised by this State is at the same time penetrated with and dominated by its class character (see how labour legislation is applied in all countries).

The extension of democracy, which Bernstein sees as a means of realizing socialism by degrees, does not contradict but, on the contrary, corresponds perfectly to the transformation realized in the nature of the State.

Konrad Schmidt declares that the conquest of a social-democratic majority in Parliament leads directly to the gradual "socialization" of society. Now, the democratic forms of political life are without a question a phenomenon clearly expressing the evolution of the State in society. They constitute, to that extent, a move toward a socialist transformation. But the conflict within the capitalist State, described above, manifests itself even more emphatically in modern parliamentarism. Indeed, in accordance with its form, parliamentarism serves to express, within the organization of the State, the interests of the whole society. But what parliamentarism expresses here is capitalist society, that is to say, a society in which capitalist interests predominate. In this society, the representative institutions, democratic in form, are in content the instruments of the interests of the ruling class. This manifests itself in a tangible fashion in the fact that as soon as democracy shows the tendency to negate its class character and become transformed into an instrument of the real interests of the population, the democratic forms are sacrificed by the bourgeoisie, and by its state representatives. That is why the idea of the conquest of a parliamentary reformist majority is a calculation which, entirely in the spirit of bourgeois liberalism, pre-occupies itself only with one side, the formal side of democracy, but does not take into account the other side, its real content. All in all, parliamentarism is not a directly socialist element impregnating gradually the whole capitalist society. It is, on the contrary, a specific form of the bourgeois class State, helping to ripen and develop the existing antagonisms of capitalism.

In the light of the history of the objective development of the State, Bernstein's and Konrad Schmidt's belief that increased "social control" results in the direct introduction of socialism is transformed into a formula that finds itself from day to day in greater contradiction with reality.

The theory of the gradual introduction of socialism proposes progressive reform of capitalist property and the capitalist State in the direction of socialism. But in consequence of the objective laws of existing society, one and the other develop in a precisely opposite direction. The process of production is increasingly socialized and State intervention, the control of the State over the process of production, is extended. But at the same time, private property becomes more and more the form of open capitalist exploitation of the labour of others and State control is penetrated with the exclusive interests of the ruling class. The State, that is to say the political organization of capitalism, and the property relations, that is to say the juridical organization of capitalism, become more capitalist and not more socialist, opposing to the theory of the progressive introduction of socialism two insurmountable difficulties.

Fourier's scheme of changing, by means of a system of phalansteries, the water of all the seas into tasty lemonade was surely a fantastic idea. But Bernstein, proposing to change the sea of capitalist bitterness into a sea of socialist sweetness, by progressively pouring into it bottles of social reformist lemonade, presents an idea that is merely more insipid but no less fantastic.

The production relations of capitalist society approach more and more the production relations of socialist society. But on the other hand, its political and juridical relations established between capitalist society and socialist society a steadily rising wall. This wall is not overthrown but is on the contrary strengthened and consolidated by the development of social reforms and the course of democracy. Only the hammer blow of revolution, that is today, the conquest of political power by the proletariat can break down this wall.

- - -

CHAPTER V.

The Consequences Of Social Reformism And General Nature Of Reformism

In the first chapter we aimed to show that Bernstein's theory lifted the program of the socialist movement off its material base and tried to place it on an idealist base. How does this theory fare when translated into practice?

Upon the first comparison, the party practice resulting from Bernstein's theory does not seem to differ from the practice followed by the Social Democracy up to now. Formerly, the activity of the Social-Democratic Party consisted of trade union work, of agitation for social reforms and the democratization of existing political institutions. The difference is not in the what, but in the how.

At present, the trade union struggle and parliamentary practice are considered to be the means of guiding and educating the proletariat in preparation for the task of taking overpower. From the revisionist standpoint, this conquest of power is at the same time impossible or useless. And therefore, trade union and parliamentary activity are to be carried on by the party only for their immediate results, that is, for the purpose of bettering the present situation of the workers, for the gradual reduction of capitalist exploitation, for the extension of social control.

So that if we do not consider momentarily the immediate amelioration of the workers' condition, an objective common to our party program as well as to revisionism, the difference between the two out-looks is, in brief, the following. According to the present conception of the party, trade-union and parliamentary activity are important for the socialist movement because such activity prepares the proletariat, that is to say, creates the subjective factor of the socialist transformation, for the task of realizing socialism. But according to Bernstein, trade-unions and parliamentary activity gradually reduce capitalist exploitation itself.

They remove from capitalist society its capitalist character. They realize objectively the desired social change.

Examining the matter closely, we see that the two conceptions are diametrically opposed. Viewing the situation from the current standpoint of our party, we say that as a result of its trade union and parliamentary struggles, the proletariat becomes convinced of the impossibility of accomplishing a fundamental social change through such activity and arrives at the understanding that the conquest of power is unavoidable. Bernstein's theory, however, begins by declaring that this conquest is impossible. It concludes by affirming that socialism can only be introduced as a result of the trade-union struggle and parliamentary activity. For as seen by Bernstein, trade union and parliamentary action has a socialist character because it exercises a progressively socializing influence on capitalist economy.

We tried to show that this influence is purely imaginary. The relations between capitalist property and the capitalist State develop in entirely opposite directions, so that the daily practical activity of the present Social Democracy loses, in the last analysis, all connection with work for socialism. From the viewpoint of a movement for socialism, the trade-union struggle and our parliamentary practice are vastly important in so far as they make socialistic the awareness, the consciousness of the proletariat and help to organize it as a class. But once they are considered as instruments of the direct socialization of capitalist economy, they lose out not only their usual effectiveness but also cease being means of preparing the working class for the conquest of power. Eduard Bernstein and Konrad Schmidt suffer from a complete misunderstanding when they console themselves with the belief that even though the program of the party is reduced to work for social reforms and ordinary trade-union work, the final objective of the labour movement is not thereby discarded, for each forward step reaches beyond the given immediate aim and the socialist goal is implied as a tendency in the supposed advance.

That is certainly true about the present procedure of the German Social Democracy. It is true whenever a firm and conscious effort for conquest of political power impregnates the trade-union struggle and the work for social reforms. But if this effort is separated from the movement itself and social reforms are made an end in themselves, then such activity not only does not lead to the final goal of socialism but moves in a precisely opposite direction.

Konrad Schmidt simply falls back on the idea that an apparently mechanical movement, once started, cannot stop by itself, because "one's appetite grows with the eating," and the working class will not supposedly content itself with reforms till the final socialist transformation is realized.

Now the last-mentioned condition is quite real. Its effectiveness is guaranteed by the very insufficiency of capitalist reforms. But the conclusion drawn from it could only be true if it were possible to construct an unbroken chain of augmented reforms leading from the capitalism of today to socialism. This is, of course, sheer fantasy. In accordance with the nature of things as they are the chain breaks quickly, and the paths that the supposed forward movement can take from the point on are many and varied.

What will be the immediate result should our party change its general procedure to suit a viewpoint that wants to emphasize the practical results of our struggle, that is social reforms? As soon as "immediate results" become the principal aim of our activity, the clear-cut, irreconcilable point of view, which has meaning only in so far as it proposes to win power, will be found more and more inconvenient. The direct consequence of this will be the adoption by the party of a "policy of compensation," a policy of political trading, and an attitude of diffident, diplomatic conciliation. But this attitude cannot be continued for a long time. Since the social reforms can only offer an empty promise, the logical consequence of such a program must necessarily be disillusionment.

It is not true that socialism will arise automatically from the daily struggle of the working class. Socialism will be the consequence of

(1) the growing contradictions of capitalist economy and

(2) of the com-prehension by the working class of the unavoidability of the suppression of these contradictions through a social transformation. When, in the manner of revisionism, the first condition is denied and the second rejected, the labour movement finds itself reduced to a simple co-operative and reformist movement. We move here in a straight line toward the total abandonment of the class viewpoint.

This consequence also becomes evident when we investigate the general character of revisionism. It is obvious that revisionism does not wish to concede that its standpoint is that of the capitalist apologist. It does not join the bourgeois economists in denying the existence of the contradictions of capitalism. But, on the other hand, what precisely constitutes the fundamental point of revisionism and distinguishes it from the attitude taken by the Social Democracy up to now, is that it does not base its theory on the belief that the contradictions of capitalism will be suppressed as a result of the logical inner development of the present economic system.

We may say that the theory of revisionism occupies an intermediate place between two extremes. Revisionism does not expect to see the contradictions of capitalism mature. It does not propose to suppress these contradictions through a revolutionary transformation. It wants to lessen, to attenuate, the capitalist contradictions. So that the antagonism existing between production and exchange is to be mollified by the cessation of crises and the formation of capitalist combines. The antagonism between Capital and Labour is to be adjusted by bettering the situation of the workers and by the conservation of the middle classes. And the contradiction between the class State and society is to be liquidated through increased State control and the progress of democracy.

It is true that the present procedure of the Social Democracy does not consist in waiting for the antagonisms of capitalism to develop and in passing on, only then, to the task of suppressing them. On the contrary, the essence of revolutionary procedure is to be guided by the direction of this development, once it is ascertained, and inferring from this direction what consequences are necessary for the political struggle. Thus, the Social Democracy has combated tariff wars and militarism without waiting for their reactionary character to become fully evident. Bernstein's procedure is not guided by a consideration of the development of capitalism, by the prospect of the aggravation of its contradictions. It is guided by the prospect of the attenuation of these contradictions. He shows this when he speaks of the "adaptation" of capitalist economy.

Now when can such a conception be correct? If it is true that capitalism will continue to develop in the direction it takes at present, then its contradictions must necessarily become sharper and more aggravated instead of disappearing. The possibility of the attenuation of the contradictions of capitalism presupposes that the capitalist mode of production itself will stop its progress. In short, the general condition of Bernstein's theory is the cessation of capitalist development.

This way, however, his theory condemns itself in a twofold manner.

In the first place, it manifests its utopian character in its stand on the establishment of socialism. For it is clear that a defective capitalist development cannot lead to a socialist transformation.

In the second place, Bernstein's theory reveals its reactionary character when it refers to the rapid capitalist development that is taking place at present. Given the development of real capitalism, how can we explain, or rather state, Bernstein's position?

We have demonstrated in the first chapter the baselessness of the economic conditions on which Bernstein builds his analysis of existing social relationships. We have seen that neither the credit system nor cartels can be said to be "means of adaptation" of capitalist economy. We have seen that not even the temporary cessation of crises nor the survival of the middle class can be regarded as symptoms of capitalist adaptation. But even though we should fail to take into account the erroneous character of all these details of Bernstein's theory we cannot help but be stopped short by one feature common to all of them. Bern-stein's theory does not seize these manifestations of contemporary economic life as they appear in their organic relationship with the whole of capitalist development, with the complete economic mechanism of capitalism. His theory pulls these details out of their living economic context. It treats them as disjecta membra (separate parts) of a lifeless machine.

Consider, for example, his conception of the adaptive effect of credit. If we recognize credit as a higher natural stage of the process of exchange and, therefore, of the contradictions inherent in capitalist exchange, we cannot at the same time see it as a mechanical means of adaptation existing outside of the process of exchange. It would be just as impossible to consider money, merchandise, and capital as "means of adaptation" of capitalism.

However, credit, like money, commodities, and capital, is an organic link of capitalist economy at a certain stage of its development. Like them, it is an indispensable gear in the mechanism of capitalist economy, and at the same time, an instrument of destruction since it aggravates the internal contradictions of capitalism.

The same thing is true about cartels and the new, perfected means of communication.

The same mechanical view is presented by Bernstein's attempt to describe the promise of the cessation of crises as a symptom of the "adaptation" of capitalist economy. For him, crises are simply derangements of the economic mechanism. With their cessation, he thinks, the mechanism could function well. But the fact is that crises are not "derangements" in the usual sense of the word. They are "derangements" without which capitalist economy could not develop at all. For if crises constitute the only method possible in capitalism and therefore the normal method of solving periodically the conflict existing between the unlimited extension of production and the narrow limits of the world market, then crises are an organic manifestation inseparable from capitalist economy.

In the "unhindered" advance of capitalist production lurks a threat to capitalism that is much greater than crises. It is the threat of the constant fall of the rate of profit, resulting not only from the contradiction between production and exchange, but from the growth of the productivity of labour itself. The fall in the rate of profit has the extremely dangerous tendency of rendering impossible any enterprise for small and middle-sized capitals. It thus limits the new formation and therefore the extension of placements of capital.

And it is precisely crises that constitute the other consequence of the same process. As a result of their periodic depreciation of capital, crises bring a fall in the prices of means of production, a paralysis of a part of the active capital and in time the increase of profits. They thus create the possibilities of the renewed advance of production. Crises therefore appear to be the instruments of rekindling the fire of capitalist development. Their cessation not temporary cessation, but their total disappearance in the world market would not lead to the further development of capitalist economy. It would destroy capitalism.

True to the mechanical view of his theory of adaptation, Bernstein forgets the necessity of crises as well as the necessity of new placements of small and middle-sized capitals. And that is why the constant reappearance of small capital seems to him to be the sign of the cessation of capitalist development though it is, in fact, a symptom of normal capitalist development.

It is important to note that there is a viewpoint from which all the above-mentioned phenomena are seen exactly as they have been presented by the theory of "adaptation." It is the viewpoint of the isolated (single) capitalist who reflects in his mind the economic facts around him just as they appear when refracted by the laws of competition. The isolated capitalist sees each organic part of the whole of our economy as an independent entity. He sees them as they act on him, the single capitalist. He therefore considers these facts to be simple "derangements" of simple "means of adaptation." For the isolated capitalist, it is true, crises are really simple derangements; the cessation of crises accords him a longer existence. As far as he is concerned, credit is only a means of "adapting" his insufficient productive forces to the needs of the market. And it seems to him that the cartel of which he becomes a member really suppresses industrial anarchy.

Revisionism is nothing else than a theoretic generalization made from the angle of the isolated capitalist. Where does this viewpoint belong theoretically if not in vulgar bourgeois economics?

All the errors of this school rest precisely on the conception that mistakes the phenomena of competition, as seen from the angle of the isolated capitalist, for the phenomena of the whole of capitalist economy. Just as Bernstein considers credit to be a means of "adaptation," to the needs of exchange. Vulgar economy, too, tries to find the antidote against the ills of capitalism in the phenomena of capitalism. Like Bernstein, it believes that it is possible to regulate capitalist economy. And in the manner of Bernstein, it arrives in time at the desire to palliate the contradictions of capitalism, that is, at the belief in the possibility of patching up the sores of capitalism. It ends up by subscribing to a program of reaction. It ends up in a utopia.

The theory of revisionism can therefore be defined in the following way. It is a theory of standing still in the socialist movement built, with the aid of vulgar economy, on a theory of capitalist standstill.

– – –

CHAPTER VI.

Economic Development And Socialism

The greatest conquest of the developing proletarian movement has been the discovery of grounds of support for the realization of socialism in the economic condition of capitalist society. As a result of this discovery, socialism was changed from an "ideal" dreamt of by humanity for thousands of years to a thing of historic necessity.

Bernstein denies the existence of the economic conditions for socialism in the society of today. On this count his reasoning has undergone an interesting evolution. At first, in the Neue Zeit, he simply contested the rapidity of the process of concentration taking place in industry. He based his position on a comparison of the occupational statistics of Germany in 1882 and 1895. In order to use these figures for his purpose, he was obliged to proceed in an entirely summary and mechanical fashion. In the most favourable case, he could not, even by demonstrating the persistence of middle-sized enterprises, weaken in any the Marxian analysis because the latter does not suppose as a condition for the realization of socialism either a definite rate of concentration of industry that is, a definite delay of the realization of socialism or, as we have already shown, the absolute disappearance of small capitals, usually described as the disappearance of the petit bourgeoisie.

In the course of the latest development of his ideas Bernstein furnishes us, in his book, a new assortment of proofs: the statistics of shareholding societies. These statistics are used in order to prove that the number of shareholders increases constantly and as a result the capitalist class does not become smaller but grows bigger. It is surprising that Bernstein has so little acquaintance with his material. And it is astonishing how poorly he utilizes the existing data in his own behalf.

If he wanted to disprove the Marxian law of industrial development by referring to the condition of shareholding societies, he should have resorted to entirely different figures. Anybody who is acquainted with the history of shareholding societies in Germany knows that their average foundation capital has diminished almost constantly. Thus, while before 1871 their average foundation capital reached the figure of 10.8 million marks, it was only 4.01 million marks in 1871, 3.8 million marks in 1873, less than a million from 1882 to 1887, 0.52 million in 1891 and only 0.62 million in 1892. After this date the figures oscillated around 1 million marks, falling to 1.78 in 1895 and to 1.19 in the course of the first half of 1897. (Van de Borght: Handwörterbuch der Staatsswissenschaften, 1.)

Those are surprising figures. Using them, Bernstein hoped to show the existence of a counter-Marxian tendency for retransformation of large enterprises into small ones. The obvious answer to his attempt is the following. If you are to prove anything at all by means of your statistics, you must first show that they refer to the same branches of industry. You must not show that small enterprises really replace large ones, that they do not. Instead, they appear only where small enterprises or even artisan industry were the rule before. This, however, you cannot show to be true. The statistical passage of immense shareholding societies to middle-size and small enterprises can be explained only by referring to the fact that the system of shareholding societies continues to penetrate new branches of production. Before, only a small number of large enterprises were organized as shareholding societies. Gradually shareholding organization has won middle-size and even small enterprises. Today we can observe shareholding societies with a capital of below 1,000 marks.

Now, what is the economic significance of the extension of the system of shareholding societies? Economically, the spread of share-holding societies stands for the growing socialization of production under the capitalist form socialization not only of large but also of middle-size and small production. The extension of shareholding does not, therefore, contradict Marxist theory but on the contrary, confirms it emphatically.

What does the economic phenomenon of a shareholding society actually amount to? It represents, on the one hand, the unification of a number of small fortunes into a large capital of production. It stands, on the other hand, for the separation of production from capitalist ownership. That is, it denotes that a double victory being won over the capitalist mode of production but still on a capitalist base.

What is the meaning, therefore, of the statistics cited by Bernstein according to which an ever-greater number of shareholders participate in capitalist enterprises? These statistics go on to precisely demonstrate the following: at present a capitalist enterprise does not correspond, as before, to a single proprietor of capital but to a number of capitalists. Consequently, the economic notion of "capitalist" no longer signifies an isolated individual. The industrial capitalist of today is a collective person composed of hundreds and even of thousands of individuals. The category "capitalist" has itself become a social category. It has become "socialized" within the framework of capitalist society.

In that case, how shall we explain Bernstein's belief that the phenomenon of share-holding societies stands for the dispersion and not the concentration of capital? Why does he see the extension of capitalist property where Marx saw its suppression?

That is a simple economic error. By "capitalist," Bernstein does not mean a category of production but the right to property. To him, "capitalist" is not an economic unit but a fiscal unit. And "capital" is for him not a factor of production but simply a certain quantity of money. That is why in his English sewing thread trust he does not see the fusion of 12,300 persons with money into a single capitalist unit but 12,300 different capitalists. That is why the engineer Schulze whose wife's dowry brought him a large number of shares from stockholder Mueller is also a capitalist for Bernstein. That is why for Bernstein the entire world seems to swarm with capitalists.

Here too, the theoretic base of his economic error is his "popularization" of socialism. For this is what he does. By transporting the concept of capitalism from its productive relations to property relations, and by speaking of simple individuals instead of speaking of entrepreneurs, he moves the question of socialism from the domain of production into the domain of relations of fortune that is, from the relation between Capital and Labour to the relation between poor and rich.

In this manner we are merrily led from Marx and Engels to the author of the Evangel of the Poor Fisherman. There is this difference, however. Weitling, with the sure instinct of the proletarian, saw in the opposition between the poor and the rich, the class antagonisms in their primitive form, and wanted to make of these antagonisms a lever of the movement for socialism. Bernstein, on the other hand, locates the realization of socialism in the possibility of making the poor rich. That is, he locates it in the attenuation of class antagonisms and therefore in the petty bourgeoisie.

True, Bernstein does not limit himself to the statistics of incomes. He furnishes statistics of economic enterprises, especially those of the following countries: Germany, France, England, Switzerland, Austria and the United States. But these statistics are not the comparative figures of different periods in each country but of each period in different countries. We are not therefore offered (with the exception of Germany where he repeats the old contrast between 1895 and 1892), a comparison of the statistics of enterprises of a given country at different epochs but the absolute figures for different countries: England in 1891, France in 1894, United States in 1890, etc.

He reaches the following conclusion: "Though it is true that large exploitation is already supreme in industry today, it nevertheless, represents, including the enterprises dependent on large exploitation, even in a country as developed in Prussia, only half of the population occupied in production." This is also true about Germany, England, Belgium, etc.

What does he actually prove here? He proves not the existence of such or such a tendency of economic development but merely the absolute relation of forces of different forms of enterprise, or put in other words, the absolute relations of the various classes in our society.

Now if one wants to prove in this manner the impossibility of realizing socialism one's reasoning must rest on the theory according to which the result of social efforts is decided by the relation of the numerical material forces of the elements in the struggle, that is, by the factor of violence. In other words, Bernstein, who always thunders against Blanquism [See: Louis Blanqui], himself falls into the grossest Blanquist error. There is this difference, however. To the Blanquists, who represented a socialist and revolutionary tendency, the possibility of the economic realization of socialism appeared quite natural. On this possibility they built the chances of a violent revolution even by a small minority. Bernstein, on the contrary, infers from the numerical insufficiency of a socialist majority, the impossibility of the economic realization of socialism. The Social-Democracy does not, however, expect to attain its aim either as a result of the victorious violence of a minority or through the numerical superiority of a majority. It sees socialism come as a result of economic necessity and the comprehension of that necessity leading to the suppression of capitalism by the working masses. And this necessity manifests itself above all in the anarchy of capitalism.

What is Bernstein's position on the decisive question of anarchy in capitalist economy? He denies only the great general crises. He does not deny partial and national crises. In other words, he refuses to see a great deal of the anarchy of capitalism; he sees only a little of it. He is to use Marx's illustration like the foolish virgin who had a child "who was only very small." But the misfortune is that in matters like economic anarchy little and much are equally bad. If Bernstein recognizes the existence of a little of this anarchy, we may point out to him that by the mechanism of the market economy this bit of anarchy will be extended to unheard of proportions, to end in collapse. But if Bernstein hopes to transform gradually his bit of anarchy into order and harmony while maintaining the system of commodity production, he again falls into one of the fundamental errors of bourgeois political economy according to which the mode of exchange is independent of the mode of production.

This is not the place for a lengthy demonstration of Bernstein's surprising confusion concerning the most elementary principles of political economy. But there is one point to which we are led by the fundamental questions of capitalist anarchy that must be clarified immediately.

Bernstein declares that Marx's law of surplus value is a simple abstraction. In political economy a statement of this sort obviously constitutes an insult. But if surplus value is only a simple abstraction, if it is only a figment of the mind then every normal citizen who has done military duty and pays his taxes on time has the same right as Karl Marx to fashion his individual absurdity, to make his own law of value. "Marx has as much right to neglect the qualities of commodities till they are no more than the incarnation of quantities of simple human labour as have the economists of the Böhm-Jevons school to make an abstraction of all the qualities of commodities outside of their utility."

That is, to Bernstein, Marx's social labour and Menger's abstract utility are quite similar pure abstractions. Bernstein forgets completely that Marx's abstraction is not an invention. It is a discovery. It does not exist in Marx's head but in market economy. It has not an imaginary existence, but a real social existence, so real that it can be cut, hammered, weighed, and put in the form of the money. The abstract human labour discovered by Marx is, in its developed form, no other than money. That is precisely one of the greatest of Marx's discoveries, while to all bourgeois political economists, from the first of the mercantilists to the last of the classicists, the essence of money has remained a mystic enigma.

The Boehm-Jevons abstract utility is, in fact, a conceit of the mind. Or stated more correctly, it is a representation of intellectual emptiness, a private absurdity, for which neither capitalism nor any other society can be made responsible, but only vulgar bourgeois economy itself. Hugging their brainchild, Bernstein, Böhm and Jevons, and the entire subjective fraternity, can remain twenty years or more before the mystery of money, without arriving at a solution that is different from the one reached by any cobbler, namely that money is also a "useful" thing.

Bernstein has lost all comprehension of Marx's law of value. Anybody with a small understanding of Marxian economics can see that without the law of value, Marx's doctrine is incomprehensible. Or to speak more concretely for him who does not understand the nature of the commodity and its exchange the entire economy of capitalism, with all its concatenations, must of necessity remain an enigma.

What precisely was the key which enabled Marx to open the door to the secrets of capitalist phenomena and solve, as if in play, problems that were not even suspected by the greatest minds of classic bourgeois economy? It was his conception of capitalist economy as an historic phenomenon not merely in the sense recognized in the best of cases by the classic economists, that is, when it concerns the feudal past of capitalism but also in so far as it concerns the socialist future of the world. The secret of Marx's theory of value, of his analysis of the problem of money, of his theory of capital, of the theory of the rate of profit and consequently of the entire existing economic system is found in the transitory character of capitalist economy, the inevitability of its collapse leading and this is only another aspect of the same phenomenon to socialism. It is only because Marx looked at capitalism from the socialist's viewpoint, that is from the historic viewpoint, that he was enabled to decipher the hieroglyphics of capitalist economy. And it is precisely because he took the socialist viewpoint as a point of departure for his analysis of bourgeois society that he was in the position to give a scientific base to the socialist movement.

This is the measure by which we evaluate Bernstein's remarks. He complains of the "dualism" found everywhere in Marx's monumental Capital. "The work wishes to be a scientific study and prove, at the same time, a thesis that was completely elaborated a long time before the editing of the book; it is based on a schema that already contains the result to which he wants to lead. The return to the Communist Manifesto (that is the socialist goal! R.L.), proves the existence of vestiges of utopianism in Marx's doctrine."

But what is Marx's "dualism" if not the dualism of the socialist future and the capitalist present? It is the dualism of Capitalism and Labour, the dualism of the bourgeoisie and the proletariat. It is the scientific reflection of the dualism existing in bourgeois society, the dualism of the class antagonism writhing inside the social order of capitalism.

Bernstein's recognition of this theoretic dualism in Marx as "a survival of utopianism" is really his naïve avowal that he denies the class antagonisms in capitalism. It is his confession that socialism has become for him only a "survival of utopianism." What is Bernstein's "monism" Bernstein's unity but the eternal unity of the capitalist regime, the unity of the former socialist who has renounced his aim and has decided to find in bourgeois society, one and immutable, the goal of human development?

Bernstein does not see in the economic structure of capitalism the development that leads to socialism. But in order to conserve his socialist program, at least in form, he is obliged to take refuge in an idealist construction placed outside of all economic development. He is obliged to transform socialism itself from a definite historical phase of social development into an abstract "principle."

That is why the "co-operative principle", the meagre decantation of socialism by which Bernstein wishes to garnish capitalist economy appears as a concession made not to the socialist future of society but to Bernstein's own socialist past.

- - -

CHAPTER VII.

Co-Operatives, Unions, Democracy

Bernstein's socialism offers to the workers the prospect of sharing in the wealth of society. The poor are to become rich. How will this socialism be brought about? His article in the Neue Zeit (Problems of Socialism) contain only vague allusions to this question. Adequate information, however, can be found in his book.

Bernstein's socialism is to be realized with the aid of these two instruments: labour unions or as Bernstein himself characterizes them, economic democracy, and co-operatives. The first will suppress industrial profit; the second will do away with commercial profit.

Co-operatives especially co-operatives in the field of production constitute a hybrid form in the midst of capitalism. They can be described as small units of socialized production within capitalist exchange.

But in capitalist economy exchanges dominate production. As a result of competition, the complete domination of the process of production by the interests of capital that is, pitiless exploitation becomes a condition for the survival of each enterprise. The domination of capital over the process of production expresses itself in the following ways. Labour is intensified. The workday is lengthened or shortened, according to the situation of the market. And, depending on the requirements of the market, labour is either employed or thrown back into the street. In other words, use is made of all methods that enable an enterprise to stand up against its competitors in the market. The workers forming a co-operative in the field of production are thus faced with the contradictory necessity of governing themselves with the utmost absolutism. They are obliged to take toward themselves the role of capitalist entrepreneur, a contradiction that accounts for the usual failure of production co-operatives which either become pure capitalist enterprises or, if the workers' interests continue to predominate end by dissolving.

Bernstein has himself taken note of these facts. But it is evident that he has not understood them. For, together with Mrs. Potter-Webb, he explains the failure of production co-operatives in England by their lack of "discipline." But what is so superficially and flatly called here "discipline" is nothing else than the natural absolutist regime of capitalism, which it is plain, the workers cannot successfully use against themselves.

Producers' co-operatives can survive within capitalist economy only if they manage to suppress, by means of some detour, the capitalist-controlled contradictions between the mode of production and the mode of exchange. And they can accomplish this only by removing themselves artificially from the influence of the laws of free competition. And they can succeed in doing the last only when they assure themselves beforehand of a constant circle of consumers, that is, when they assure themselves of a constant market.

It is the consumers' co-operative that can offer this service to its brother in the field of production. Here and not in Oppenheimer's distinction between co-operatives that produce and co-operatives that sell is the secret sought by Bernstein: the explanation for the invariable failure of producers' co-operatives functioning independently and their survival when they are backed by consumers' organizations.

If it is true that the possibilities of existence of producers' co-operatives within capitalism are bound up with the possibilities of existence of consumers' co-operatives, then the scope of the former is limited, in the most favourable of cases, to the small local market and to the manufacture of articles serving immediate needs, especially food products. Consumers' and therefore producers' co-operatives, are excluded from the most important branches of capital production the textile, mining, metallurgical and petroleum industries, machine construction, locomotive and shipbuilding. For this reason alone (forgetting for the moment their hybrid character), co-operatives in the field of production cannot be seriously considered as the instrument of a general social transformation. The establishment of producers' co-operatives on a wide scale would suppose first of all, the suppression of the world market, the breaking up of the present world economy into small local spheres of production and exchange. The highly developed, widespread capitalism of our time is expected to fall back to the merchant economy of the Middle Ages.

Within the framework of present society, producers' co-operatives are limited to the role of simple annexes to consumers' co-operatives. It appears, therefore, that the latter must be the beginning of the proposed social change. But this way the expected reform of society by means of co-operatives ceases to be an offensive against capitalist production. That is, it ceases to be an attack against the principal bases of capitalist economy. It becomes, instead, a struggle against commercial capital, especially small and middle-sized commercial capital. It becomes an attack made on the twigs of the capitalist tree.

According to Bernstein, trade unions too, are a means of attack against capitalism in the field of production. We have already shown that trade unions cannot give the workers a determining influence over production. Trade unions can determine neither the dimensions of pro-duction nor the technical progress of production.

This much may be said about the purely economic side of the "struggle of the rate of wages against the rate of profit," as Bernstein labels the activity of the trade union. It does not take place in the blue of the sky.

It takes place within the well-defined framework of the law of wages. The law of wages is not shattered but applied by trade-union activity.

According to Bernstein, it is the trade unions that lead in the general movement for the emancipation of the working class, the real attack against the rate of industrial profit. According to Bernstein, trade unions have the task of transforming the rate of industrial profit into "rates of wages." The fact is that trade unions are least able to execute an economic offensive against profit. Trade unions are nothing more than the organized defence of labour power against the attacks of profit. They express the resistance offered by the working class to the oppression of capitalist economy.

On the one hand, trade unions have the function of influencing the situation in the labour power market. But this influence is being constantly overcome by the proletarianization of the middle layers of our society, a process which continually brings new merchandise on the labour market. The second function of the trade unions is to ameliorate the condition of the workers. That is, they attempt to increase the share of the social wealth going to the working class. This share, however, is being reduced with the fatality of a natural process by the growth of the productivity of labour. One does not need to be a Marxist to notice this. It suffices to read Rodbertus' in Explanation of the Social Question.

In other words, the objective conditions of capitalist society transform the two economic functions of the trade unions into a sort of labour of Sisyphus[1], which is, nevertheless, indispensable. For as a result of the activity of his trade unions, the worker succeeds in obtaining for himself the rate of wages due to him in accordance with the situation of the labour-power market. As a result of trade union activity, the capitalist law of wages is applied and the effect of the depressing tendency of economic development is paralyzed, or to be more exact, attenuated.

1. The mythological king of Corinth who was condemned to roll a huge stone to the top of a hill. It constantly rolled back down against making his task incessant.

However, the transformation of the trade union into an instrument for the progressive reduction of profit in favour of wages presupposes the following social conditions; first, the cessation of the proletarianization of the middle strata of our society; secondly, a stoppage of the growth of productivity of labour. We have in both cases a return to pre-capitalist conditions, Co-operatives and trade unions are totally incapable of transforming the capitalist mode of production. This is really understood by Bernstein, though in a confused manner. For he refers to co-operatives and trade unions as a means of reducing the profit of the capitalists and thus enriching the workers. In this way, he renounces the struggle against the capitalist mode of production and attempts to direct the socialist movement to struggle against "capitalist distribution." Again and again, Bernstein refers to socialism as an effort towards a "just, Juster and still more just" mode of distribution. (Vorwärts, March 26, 1899).

It cannot be denied that the direct cause leading the popular masses into the socialist movement is precisely the "unjust" mode of distribution characteristic of capitalism. When the Social-Democracy struggles for the socialization of the entire economy, it aspires therewith also to a "just" distribution of the social wealth. But, guided by Marx's observation that the mode of distribution of a given epoch is a natural consequence of the mode of production of that epoch, the Social-Democracy does not struggle against distribution in the framework of capitalist production. It struggles instead for the suppression of the capitalist production itself. In a word, the Social-Democracy wants to establish the mode of socialist distribution by suppressing the capitalist mode of production. Bernstein's method, on the contrary, proposes to combat the capitalist mode of distribution in the hopes of gradually establishing, in this way, the socialist mode of production.

What, in that case, is the basis of Bernstein's program for the reform of society? Does it find support in definite tendencies of capitalist production? No. In the first place, he denies such tendencies. In the second place, the socialist transformation of production is for him the effect and not the cause of distribution. He cannot give his program a materialist base because he has already overthrown the aims and the means of the movement for socialism, and therefore its economic conditions. As a result, he is obliged to construct himself an idealist base.

"Why represent socialism as the consequence of economic compulsion?" he complains. "Why degrade man's understanding, his feeling for justice, his will?" (Vorwärts, March 26, 1899). Bernstein's superlatively just distribution is to be attained thanks to man's free will man's will acting not because of economic necessity, since this will be only an instrument, but because of man's comprehension of justice, because of man's idea of justice.

We thus quite happily return to the principle of justice, to the old war horse on which the reformers of the earth have rocked for ages, for the lack of surer means of historic transportation. We return to the lamentable Rosinate on which the Don Quixotes of history have galloped towards the great reform of the earth, always to come home with their eyes blackened.

The relation of the poor to the rich, taken as a base for socialism, the principle of co-operation as the content of socialism, the "most just distribution" as its aim, and the idea of justice as its only historic legitimization with how much more force, more with and more fire did Weitling defend that sort of socialism fifty years ago. However, that genius of a tailor did not know scientific socialism. If today, the conception tore into bits by Marx and Engels a half century ago is patched up and presented to the proletariat as the last world of social science, that too, is the art of a tailor but it has nothing of a genius about it.

Trade unions and co-operatives are the economic support for the theory of revisionism. Its principal political condition is the growth of democracy. The present manifestations of political reaction are to Bernstein only "displacement." He considers them accidental, momentary, and suggests that they are not to be considered in the elaboration of the general directives of the labour movement.

To Bernstein, democracy is an inevitable stage in the development of society. To him, as to the bourgeois theoreticians of liberalism, democracy is the great fundamental law of historic development, the realization of which is served by all the forces of political life. However, Bernstein's thesis is completely false. Presented in this absolute force, it appears as a petty-bourgeois vulgarization of results of a very short phase of bourgeois development, the last twenty-five or thirty years. We reach entirely different conclusions when we examine the historic development of democracy a little closer and consider, at the same time, the general political history of capitalism.

Democracy has been found in the most dissimilar social formations in primitive communist groups, in the slave states of antiquity and in medieval communes. And similarly, absolutism and constitutional monarchy are to be found under the most varied economic orders. When capitalism began, with the first production of commodities, it resorted to a democratic constitution in the municipal communes of the Middle Ages. Later, when it developed to manufacturing, capitalism found its corresponding political form in the absolute monarchy. Finally, as a developed industrial economy, it brought into being in France the democratic republic of 1793, the absolute monarchy of Napoleon I, the nobles' monarchy of the Restoration period (1850-1830), the bourgeois constitutional monarchy of Louis-Philippe then again, the democratic republic, and against the monarchy of Napoleon III and finally, for the third time, the Republic.

In Germany, the only truly democratic institution universal suffrage is not a conquest won by bourgeois liberalism. Universal suffrage in Germany was an instrument for the fusion of the small States. It is only in this sense that it has any importance for the development of the German bourgeoisie, which is otherwise quite satisfied with semi-feu-dal constitutional monarchy. In Russia, capitalism prospered for a long time under the regime of oriental absolutism, without having the bourgeoisie manifest the least desire in the world to introduce democracy. In Austria, universal suffrage was above all a safety line thrown to a foundering and decomposing monarchy. In Belgium, the conquest of universal suffrage by the labour movement was undoubtedly due to the weakness of the local militarism, and consequently to the special geo-graphic and political situation of the country. But we have here a "bit of democracy" that has been won not by the bourgeoisie but against it.

The uninterrupted victory of democracy, which to our revisionism as well as to bourgeois liberalism, appears as a great fundamental law of human history and, especially, modern history is shown upon closer examination to be a phantom. No absolute and general relation can be constructed between capitalist development and democracy. The political form of a given country is always the result of the composite of all the existing political factors, domestic as well as foreign. It admits within its limits all variations of the scale from absolute monarchy to the democratic republic.

We must abandon, therefore, all hope of establishing democracy as a general law of historical development even within the framework of modern society. Turning to the present phase of bourgeois society, we observe here, too, political factors which, instead of assuring the realization of Bernstein's schema, led rather to the abandonment by bourgeois society of the democratic conquests won up to now.

Democratic institutions and this is of the greatest significance have completely exhausted their function as aids in the development of bourgeois society. In so far as they were necessary to bring about the fusion of small States and the creation of large modern States (Germany, Italy), they are no longer indispensable at present. Economic development has meanwhile affected an internal organic cicatrisation.

The same thing can be said concerning the transformation of the entire political and administrative State machinery from feudal or semi-feudal mechanism to capitalist mechanism. While this trans-formation has been historically inseparable from the development of democracy, it has been realized today to such an extent that the purely democratic "ingredients" of society, such as universal suffrage and the republican State form, may be suppressed without having the administration, the State finances, or the military organization find it necessary to return to the forms they had before the March Revolution[2].

If liberalism as such is now absolutely useless to bourgeois society it has become, on the other hand, a direct impediment to capitalism from other standpoints. Two factors dominate completely the political life of contemporary States: world politics and the labour movement. Each is only a different aspect of the present phase of capitalist development.

As a result of the development of the world economy and the aggravation and generalization of competition on the world market, militarism and the policy of big navies have become, as instruments of world politics, a decisive factor in the interior as well as in the exterior life of the great States. If it is true that world politics and militarism rep-resent a rising tendency in the present phase of capitalism, then bourgeois democracy must logically move in a descending line.

In Germany the era of great armament, began in 1893, and the policy of world politics inaugurated with the seizure of Kiao-Cheou were paid for immediately with the following sacrificial victim: the decomposition of liberalism, the deflation of the Centre Party, which passed from opposition to government. The recent elections to the Reichstag of 1907 unrolling under the sign of the German colonial policy were, at the same time, the historical burial of German liberalism.

If foreign politics push the bourgeoisie into the arms of reaction this is no less true about domestic politics thanks to the rise of the working class. Bernstein shows that he recognizes this when he makes the social-democratic "legend," which "wants to swallow everything", in other words, the socialist efforts of the working class responsible for the desertion of the liberal bourgeoisie. He advises the proletariat to disavow its socialist aim so that the mortally frightened liberals might

2. The German revolution of 1848, which struck an effective blow against the feudal institutions in Germany.

come out of the mouse hole of reaction. Making the suppression of the socialist labour movement an essential condition for the preservation of bourgeois democracy, he proves in a striking manner that this democracy is in complete contradiction with the inner tendency of development of the present society. He proves, at the same time, that the socialist movement is itself a direct product of this tendency.

But he proves, at the same time, still another thing. By making the denouncement of the socialist aim an essential condition of the resurrection of bourgeois democracy, he shows how inexact is the claim that bourgeois democracy is an indispensable condition of the socialist movement and the victory of socialism. Bernstein's reasoning exhausts itself in a vicious circle. His conclusion swallows his premises.

The solution is quite simple. In view of that fact that bourgeois liberalism has given up its ghost from fear of the growing labour movement and its final aim, we conclude that the socialist labour movement is today the only support for that which is not the goal of the socialist movement democracy. We must conclude that democracy can have no support. We must conclude that the socialist movement is not bound to bourgeois democracy but that, on the contrary, the fate of democracy is bound up with the socialist movement. We must conclude from this that democracy does not acquire greater chances of survival, as the socialist movement becomes sufficiently strong to struggle against the reactionary consequences of world politics and the bourgeois desertion of democracy. He who would strengthen democracy should want to strengthen and not weaken the socialist movement. He who renounces the struggle for socialism renounces both the labour movement and democracy.

– – –

CHAPTER VIII.

Conquest Of Political Power

The fate of democracy is bound up, we have seen, with the fate of the labour movement. But does the development of democracy render superfluous or impossible a proletarian revolution, that is, the conquest of political power by the workers?

Bernstein settles the question by weighing minutely the good and bad sides of social reform and social revolution. He does it almost in the same manner in which cinnamon or pepper is weighed out in a consumers' co-operative store. He sees the legislative course of historic development as the action of "intelligence," while the revolutionary course of historic development is for him the action of "feeling." Reformist activity, he recognizes as a slow method of historic progress, revolution as a rapid method of progress. In legislation he sees a methodical force, in revolution, a spontaneous force.

We have known for a long time that the petty-bourgeoisie reformer finds "good" and "bad" sides in everything. He nibbles a bit at all grasses. But the real course of events is little affected by such com-bination. The carefully gathered little pile of the "good sides" of all thing's possible collapses at the first flip of history. Historically, legislative reform and the revolutionary method function in accordance with influences that are much more profound than the consideration of the advantages or inconveniences of one method or another.

In the history of bourgeois society, legislative reform served to strengthen progressively the rising class till the latter was sufficiently strong to seize political power, to suppress the existing juridical system and to construct itself a new one. Bernstein, thundering against the conquest of political power as a theory of Blanquist violence, has the misfortune of labelling as a Blanquist error that which has always been the pivot and the motive force of human history. From the first appearance of class societies having the class struggle as the essential content of their history, the conquest of political power has been the aim of all rising classes. Here is the starting point and end of every historic period. This can be seen in the long struggle of the Latin peasantry against the financiers and nobility of ancient Rome, in the struggle of the medieval nobility against the bishops and in the struggle of the artisans against the nobles, in the cities of the Middle Ages. In modern times, we see it in the struggle of the bourgeoisie against feudalism.

Legislative reform and revolution are not different methods of historic development that can be picked out at the pleasure from the counter of history, just as one chooses hot or cold sausages. Legislative reform and revolution are different factors in the development of class society. They condition and complement each other and are at the same time reciprocally exclusive, as are the north and south poles, the bourgeoisie and proletariat.

Every legal constitution is the product of a revolution. In the history of classes, revolution is the act of political creation, while legislation is the political expression of the life of a society that has already come into being. Work for reform does not contain its own force independent from revolution. During every historic period, work for reforms is carried on only in the direction given to it by the impetus of the last revolution and continues as long as the impulsion from the last revolution continues to make itself felt. Or, to put it more concretely, in each historic period work for reforms is carried on only in the framework of the social form created by the last revolution. Here is the kernel of the problem.

It is contrary to history to represent work for reforms as a long-drawn out revolution and revolution as a condensed series of reforms. A social transformation and a legislative reform do not differ according to their duration but according to their content. The secret of historic change through the utilization of political power resides precisely in the transformation of simple quantitative modification into a new quality, or to speak more concretely, in the passage of an historic period from one given form of society to another.

That is why people who pronounce themselves in favour of the method of legislative reform in place and in contradistinction to the conquest of political power and social revolution, do not really choose a more tranquil, calmer, and slower road to the same goal, but a different goal. Instead of taking a stand for the establishment of a new society they take a stand for surface modifications of the old society. If we follow the political conceptions of revisionism, we arrive at the same conclusion that is reached when we follow the economic theories of revisionism. Our program becomes not the realization of socialism, but the reform of capitalism; not the suppression of the wage labour system but the diminution of exploitation, that is, the suppression of the abuses of capitalism instead of suppression of capitalism itself.

Does the reciprocal role of legislative reform and revolution apply only to the class struggle of the past? It is possible that now, as a result of the development of the bourgeois juridical system, the function of moving society from one historic phase to another belongs to legislative reform and that the conquest of State power by the proletariat has really become "an empty phrase," as Bernstein puts it?

The very opposite is true. What distinguishes bourgeois society from other class societies from ancient society and from the social order of the Middle Ages? Precisely the fact that class domination does not rest on "acquired rights" but on real economic relations, the fact that wage labour is not a juridical relation, but purely an economic relation. In our juridical system there is not a single legal formula for the class domination of today. The few remaining traces of such formulae of class domination are (as that concerning servants), survivals of feudal society.

How can wage slavery be suppressed the "legislative way," if wage slavery is not expressed the laws? Bernstein, who would do away with capitalism by means of legislative reforms, finds himself in the same situation as Uspensky's Russian policeman who said: "Quickly I seized the rascal by the collar! But what do I see? The confounded fellow has no collar!" And that is precisely Bernstein's difficulty.

"All previous societies were based on an antagonism between an oppressing class and an oppressed class" (Communist Manifesto). But in the preceding phases of modern society, this antagonism was expressed in distinctly determined juridical relations and could, especially because of that, accord, to a certain extent, a place to new relations within the framework of the old. "In the midst of serfdom, the serf raised him-self to the rank of a member of the town community" (Communist Manifesto). How was that made possible? It was made possible by the progressive of all feudal privileges in the environs of the city: the corvée, the right to special dress, the inheritance tax, the lord's claim to the best cattle, the personal levy, marriage under duress, the right to succession, etc., which all together constituted serfdom.

In the same way, the small bourgeoisie of the Middle Ages succeeded in raising itself, while it was still under the yoke of feudal absolutism, to the rank of bourgeoisie (Communist Manifesto). By what means? By means of the formal partial suppression or complete loosening of the corporative bonds, by the progressive transformation of the fiscal administration and of the army.

Consequently, when we consider the question from the abstract viewpoint, not from the historic viewpoint, we can imagine (in view of the former class relations) a legal passage, according to the reformist method, from feudal society to bourgeois society. But what do we see in reality? In reality, we see that legal reforms not only do not obviate the seizure of political power by the bourgeoisie but have, on the contrary, prepared for it and led to it. A formal social-political transformation was indispensable for the abolition of slavery as well as for the complete suppression of feudalism.

But the situation is entirely different now. No law obliges the proletariat to submit itself to the yoke of capitalism. Poverty, the lack of means of production, obliges the proletariat to submit itself to the yoke of capitalism. And no law in the world can give to the proletariat the means of production while it remains in the framework of bourgeois society, for not laws but economic development have torn the means of production from the producers' possession.

And neither is the exploitation inside the system of wage labour based on laws. The level of wages is not fixed by legislation but by economic factors. The phenomenon of capitalist exploitation does not rest on a legal disposition but on the purely economic fact that labour power plays in this exploitation the role of a merchandise possessing, among other characteristics, the agreeable quality of producing value more than the value it consumes in the form of the labourer's means of subsistence. In short, the fundamental relations of the domination of the capitalist class cannot be transformed by means of legislative reforms, on the basis of capitalist society, because these relations have not been introduced by bourgeois laws, nor have they received the form of such laws. Apparently, Bernstein is not aware of this for he speaks of "socialist reforms." On the other hand, he seems to express implicit recognition of this when he writes, on page 10 of his book, "the economic motive acts freely today, while formerly it was masked by all kinds of relations of domination by all sorts of ideology."

It is one of the peculiarities of the capitalist order that within it all the elements of the future society first assume, in their development, a form not approaching socialism but, on the contrary, a form moving more and more away from socialism. Production takes on a progressively increasing social character. But under what form is the social character of capitalist production expressed? It is expressed in the form of the large enterprise, in the form of the shareholding concern, the cartel, within which the capitalist antagonisms, capitalist exploitation, the oppression of labour-power, are augmented to the extreme.

In the army, capitalist development leads to the extension of obligatory military service to the reduction of the time of service and consequently to a material approach to a popular militia. But all of this takes place under the form of modern militarism in which the domination of the people by the militarist State and the class character of the State manifest themselves most clearly.

In the field of political relations, the development of democracy brings in the measure that it finds a favourable soil, the participation of all popular strata in political life and, consequently, some sort of "people's State." But this participation takes the form of bourgeois parliamentarism, in which class antagonisms and class domination are not done away with, but are, on the contrary, displayed in the open. Exactly because capitalist development moves through these contradictions, it is necessary to extract the kernel of socialist society from its capitalist shell. Exactly for this reason must the proletariat seize political power and suppress completely the capitalist system.

Of course, Bernstein draws other conclusions. If the development of democracy leads to the aggravation and not to the lessening of capitalist antagonisms, "the Social-Democracy," he answers us, "in order not to render its task more difficult, must by all means try to stop social reforms and the extension of democratic institutions," (page 71). Indeed, that would be the right thing to do if the Social-Democracy found to its taste, in the petty-bourgeois manner, the futile task of picking for itself all the good sides of history and rejecting the bad sides of history. However, in that case, it should at the same time "try to stop" capitalism in general, for there is no doubt that the latter is the rascal placing all these obstacles in the way of socialism. But capitalism furnishes besides the obstacles also the only possibilities of realizing the socialist programme. The same can be said about democracy.

If democracy has become superfluous or annoying to the bourgeoisie, it is on the contrary necessary and indispensable to the working class. It is necessary to the working class because it creates the political forms (autonomous administration, electoral rights, etc.) which will serve the proletariat as fulcrums in its task of transforming bourgeois society. Democracy is indispensable to the working class because only through the exercise of its democratic rights, in the struggle for democracy, can the proletariat become aware of its class interests and its historic task.

In a word, democracy is indispensable not because it renders superfluous the conquest of political power by the proletariat but because it renders this conquest of power both necessary and possible. When Engels, in his preface to the Class Struggles in France, revised the tactics of the modern labour movement and urged the legal struggle as opposed to the barricades, he did not have in mind this comes out of every line of the preface, the question of a definite conquest of political power but the contemporary daily struggle. He did not have in mind the attitude that the proletariat must take toward the capitalist State at the time of the seizure of power but the attitude of the proletariat while in the bounds of the capitalist State. Engels was giving directions to the proletariat oppressed, and not to the proletariat victorious.

On the other hand, Marx's well-known sentence on the agrarian question in England (Bernstein leans on it heavily), in which he says: "We shall probably succeed easier by buying the estates of the landlords," does not refer to the stand of the proletariat before, but after its victory. For there, evidently can be a question of buying the property of the old dominant class only when the workers are in power. The possibility envisaged by Marx is that of the pacific exercise of the dictatorship of the proletariat and not the replacement of the dictatorship with capitalist social reforms. There was no doubt for Marx and Engels about the necessity of having the proletariat conquer political power. It is left to Bernstein to consider the poultry-yard of bourgeois parliamentarism as the organ by means of which we are to realize the most formidable social transformation of history, the passage from capitalist society to socialism.

Bernstein introduces his theory by warning the proletariat against the danger of acquiring power too early. That is, according to Bernstein, the proletariat ought to leave the bourgeois society in its present condition and itself suffer a frightful defeat. If the proletariat came to power, it could draw from Bernstein's theory the following "practical" conclusion to go to sleep. His theory condemns the proletariat at the most decisive moments of the struggle, to inactivity, to a passive betrayal of its own cause.

Our programme would be a miserable scrap of paper if it could not serve us in all eventualities, at all moments of the struggle and if it did not serve us by its application and not by its non-application. If our programme contains the formula of the historical development of society from capitalism to socialism, it must also formulate, in all its characteristic fundamentals, all the transitory phases of this development and it should, consequently, be able to indicate to the proletariat what ought to be its corresponding action at every moment on the road toward socialism. There can be no time for the proletariat when it will be obliged to abandon its programme or be abandoned by it.

Practically, this is manifested in the fact that there can be no time when the proletariat, placed in power by the force of events, is not in the condition or is not morally obliged to take certain measures for the realization of its programme, that is, take transitory measures in the direction of socialism. Behind the belief that the socialist programme can collapse completely at any point of the dictatorship of the proletariat lurks the other belief that the socialist programme is generally and at all times, unrealizable.

And what if the transitory measures are premature? The question hides a great number of mistaken ideas concerning the real course of a social transformation.

In the first place, the seizure of political power by the proletariat, that is to say by a large popular class, is not produced artificially. It presupposes (with the exception of such cases as the Paris Commune, when the proletariat did not obtain power after a conscious struggle for its goal but fell into its hands like a good thing abandoned by everybody else) a definite degree of maturity of economic and political relations. Here we have the essential difference between coups d'etat along Blan-qui's conception which are accomplished by an "active minority" and burst out like pistol shot, always inopportunely, and the conquest of political power by a great conscious popular mass which can only be the product of the decomposition of bourgeois society and therefore bears in itself the economic and political legitimization of its opportune appearance.

If, therefore, considered from the angle of political effect the conquest of political power by the working class cannot materialize itself "too early" then from the angle of conservation of power, the premature revolution, the thought of which keeps Bernstein awake, menaces us like a sword of Damocles. Against that neither prayers nor supplication, neither scares nor any amount of anguish, are of any avail. And this for two very simple reasons.

In the first place, it is impossible to imagine that a transformation as formidable as the passage from capitalist society to socialist society can be realized in one happy act. To consider that as possible is, again, to lend colour to conceptions that are clearly Blanquist. The socialist transformation supposes a long and stubborn struggle, in the course of which, it is quite probable the proletariat will be repulsed more than once so that for the first time, from the viewpoint of the final outcome of the struggle, it will have necessarily come to power "too early."

In the second place, it will be impossible to avoid the "premature" conquest of State power by the proletariat precisely because these "premature" attacks of the proletariat constitute a factor and indeed a very important factor, creating the political conditions of the final victory. In the course of the political crisis accompanying its seizure of power, in the course of the long and stubborn struggles, the proletariat will acquire the degree of political maturity permitting it to obtain in time a definitive victory of the revolution. Thus these "premature" attacks of the proletariat against the State power are in themselves important historic factors helping to provoke and determine the point of the definite victory. Considered from this viewpoint, the idea of a "premature" conquest of political power by the labouring class appears to be a polemic absurdity derived from a mechanical conception of the development of society and positing for the victory of the class struggle a point fixed outside and independent of the class struggle.

Since the proletariat is not in the position to seize power in any other way than "prematurely," since the proletariat is absolutely obliged to seize power once or several times "too early" before it can maintain itself in power for good, the objection to the "premature" conquest of power is at bottom nothing more than a general opposition to the aspiration of the proletariat to possess itself of State power. Just as all roads lead to Rome so too do, we logically arrive at the conclusion that the revisionist proposal to slight the final aim of the socialist movement is really a recommendation to renounce the socialist movement itself.

- - -

CHAPTER IX.

Collapse

Bernstein began his revision of the Social-Democracy by abandoning the theory of capitalist collapse. The latter, however, is the cornerstone of scientific socialism. By rejecting it Bernstein also rejects the whole doctrine of socialism. In the course of his discussion, he abandons one after another of the positions of socialism in order to be able to maintain his first affirmation.

Without the collapse of capitalism, the expropriation of the capitalist class is impossible. Bernstein therefore renounces expropriation and chooses a progressive realization of the "co-operative principle" as the aim of the labour movement.

But co-operation cannot be realized without capitalist production. Bernstein, therefore, renounces the socialization of production and merely proposes to reform commerce and to develop consumers' co-operatives.

But the transformation of society through consumers' co-operatives, even by means of trade unions, is incompatible with the real material development of capitalist society. Therefore, Bernstein abandons the materialist conception of history.

But his conception of the march of economic development is incompatible with the Marxist theory of surplus-value. Therefore,

Bernstein abandons the theory of value and surplus-value and in this way, the whole economic system of Karl Marx.

But the struggle of the proletariat cannot be carried on without a given final aim and without an economic base found in the existing society. Bernstein, therefore, abandons the class struggle and speaks of reconciliation with bourgeois liberalism.

But in a class society, the class struggle is a natural and unavoidable phenomenon. Bernstein, therefore, contests even the existence of classes in society. The working class is for him a mass of individuals, divided politically and intellectually but also economically. And the bourgeoisie, according to him, does not group itself politically in accordance with its inner economic interest but only because of exterior pressure from above and below.

But if there is no economic base for the class struggle and, if consequently, there are no classes in our society, not only the future but even the past struggles of the proletariat against the bourgeoisie appear to be impossible and the Social-Democracy and its successes seem absolutely incomprehensible or they can be understood only as the results of political pressure by the government that is, not as the natural consequence of historic development but as the fortuitous consequences of the policy of the Hohenzollern not as the legitimate offspring of capitalist society but as the legitimate offspring of capitalist society but as the bastard children of reaction. Rigorously logical, in this respect, Bernstein passes from the materialist conception of history to the outlook of the Frankfurter Zeitung and the Vossische Zeitung.

After rejecting the socialist criticism of capitalist society, it is easy for Bernstein to find the present state of affairs satisfactory at least in a general way. Bernstein does not hesitate. He discovers that at the present time reaction is not very strong in Germany, that "we cannot speak of political reaction in the countries of western Europe," and that in all the countries of the West "the attitude of the bourgeois classes toward the socialist movement is at most an attitude of defence and not one of oppression," (Vorwärts, March 26, 1899). Far from becoming worse, the situation of the workers is getting better. Indeed, the bourgeoisie is politically progressive and morally sane. We cannot speak either of reaction or oppression. It is all for the best in the best of all possible worlds…

Bernstein thus travels in logical sequence from A to Z. He began by abandoning the final aim and supposedly keeping the movement. But as there can be no socialist movement without a socialist aim he ends by renouncing the movement.

And thus, the Bernstein's conception of socialism collapses entirely. The proud and admirable symmetric construction of socialist thought becomes for him a pile of rubbish in which the debris of all systems, the pieces of thought of various great and small minds, find a common resting place. Marx and Proudhon, Leon von Buch and Franz Oppenheimer, Friedrich Albert Lange and Kant, Herr Prokopovich and R. Ritter von Neupauer, Herkner, and Schulze-Gävernitz, Lassalle and Professor Julius Wolff: all contribute something to Bernstein's system. From each he takes a little. There is nothing astonishing about that. For when he abandoned scientific socialism, he lost the axis of intellectual crystallization around which isolated facts group themselves in the organic whole of a coherent conception of the world.

His doctrine, composed of bits of all possible systems, seems upon first consideration to be completely free from prejudices. For Bernstein does not like talk of "party science," or to be more exact, of class science, any more than he likes to talk of class liberalism or class morality. He thinks he succeeds in expressing human, general, abstract science, abstract liberalism, abstract morality. But since the society of reality is made up of classes which have diametrically opposed interests, aspirations and conceptions, a general human science in social questions, an abstract liberalism, an abstract morality, are at present illusions, pure utopia. The science, the democracy, the morality, considered by Bernstein as general, human, are merely the dominant science, dominant democracy and dominant morality that is, bourgeois science, bourgeois democracy, bourgeois morality.

When Bernstein rejects the economic doctrine of Marx in order to swear by the teachings of Bretano, Böhm-Bawerk, Jevons, Say and Julius Wolff, he exchanges the scientific base of the emancipation of the working class for the apologetics of the bourgeoisie. When he speaks of the generally human character of liberalism and transforms socialism into a variety of liberalism, he deprives the socialist movement (generally) of its class character and consequently of its historic content, consequently of all content and conversely, recognizes the class representing liberalism in history, the bourgeoisie, as the champion of the general interests of humanity.

And when he wars against "raising of the material factors to the rank of an all-powerful force of development," when he protests against the so-called "contempt for the ideal" that is supposed to rule the Social-Democracy, when he presumes to talk for idealism, for morals, pronouncing himself at the same time against the only source of the moral rebirth of the proletariat, a revolutionary class struggle, he does no more than the following: preach to the working class the quintessence of the morality of the bourgeoisie, that is, reconciliation with the existing social order and the transfer of the hopes of the proletariat to the limbo of ethical simulacra.

When he directs his keenest arrows against our dialectic system, he is really attacking the specific mode of thought employed by the conscious proletariat in its struggle for liberation. It is an attempt to break the sword that has helped the proletariat to pierce the darkness of its future. It is an attempt to shatter the intellectual arm with the aid of which the proletariat, though materially under the yoke of the bourgeoisie, is yet enabled to triumph over the bourgeoisie. For it is our dialectical system that shows to the working class the transitory nature of this yoke, proving to workers the inevitability of their victory and is already realizing a revolution in the domain of thought. Saying good-bye to our system of dialectics and resorting instead to the intellectual seesaw of the well-known "on the one hand on the other hand," "yes but," "although however," "more less," etc., he quite logically lapses into a mode of thought that belongs historically to the bourgeoisie in decline, being the faithful intellectual reflection of the social existence and political activity of the bourgeoisie at that stage. The political "on the one hand, on the other hand," "yes but" of the bourgeoisie today resembles, in a marked degree, Bernstein's manner of thinking which is the sharpest and surest proof of the bourgeois nature of his conception of the world.

But, as it us used by Bernstein, the word "bourgeois" itself is not a class expression but a general social notion. Logical to the end he has exchanged, together with his science, politics, morals and mode of thinking, the historic language of the proletariat for that of the bourgeoisie. When he uses, without distinction, the term "citizen" in reference to the bourgeois as well as to the proletarian intending, thereby, to refer to man in general, he identifies man in general with the bourgeois and human society with bourgeois society.

– – –

CHAPTER X.

Opportunism And Theory In Practice

Bernstein's book is of great importance to the German and the international labour movement. It is the first attempt to give a theoretic base to the opportunist currents common in the Social-Democracy.

These currents may be said to have existed for a long time in our movement if we take into consideration such sporadic manifestations of opportunism as the question of subsidization of steamers. But it is only since about 1890, with the suppression of the anti-Socialist laws, that we have had a trend of opportunism of a clearly defined character. Vollmar's "State Socialism," the vote on the Bavarian budget, the "agrarian socialism" of south Germany, Heine's policy of compensation, Schippel's stand on tariffs and militarism, are the high points in the development of our opportunist practice.

What appears to characterize this practice above all? A certain hostility to "theory." This is quite natural, for our "theory," that is, the principles of scientific socialism, impose clearly marked limitations to practical activity insofar as it concerns the aims of this activity, the means used in attaining these aims and the method employed in this activity. It is quite natural for people who run after immediate "practical" results to want to free themselves from such limitations and to render their practice independent of our "theory."

However, this outlook is refuted by every attempt to apply it in reality.

State socialism, agrarian socialism, the policy of compensation, the question of the army, all constituted defeats to our opportunism. It is clear that, if this current is to maintain itself, it must try to destroy the principles of our theory and elaborate a theory of its own. Bernstein's book is precisely an effort in that direction. That is why at Stuttgart all the opportunist elements in our party immediately grouped themselves around Bernstein's banner. If the opportunist currents in the practical activity of our party are an entirely natural phenomenon which can be explained in the light of the special conditions of our activity and its development, Bernstein's theory is no less natural an attempt to group these currents into a general theoretic expression, an attempt to elaborate its own theoretic conditions and the break with scientific socialism. That is why the published expression of Bernstein's ideas should be recognized as a theoretic test for opportunism and as its first scientific legitimization.

What was the result of this test? We have seen the result. Opportunism is not a position to elaborate a positive theory capable of with-standing criticism. All it can do is to attack various isolated theses of Marxist theory and, just because Marxist doctrine constitutes one sol-idly constructed edifice, hope by this means to shake the entire system from the top to its foundation.

This shows that opportunist practice is essentially irreconcilable with Marxism. But it also proves that opportunism is incompatible with socialism (the socialist movement) in general, that its internal tendency is to push the labour movement into bourgeois paths, that opportunism tends to paralyze completely the proletarian class struggle. The latter, considered historically, has evidently nothing to do with Marxist doctrine. For, before Marx and independently from him, there have been labour movements and various socialist doctrines, each of which, in its way, was the theoretic expression corresponding to the conditions of the time, of the struggle of the working class for emancipation. The theory that consists in basing socialism on the moral notion of justice, on a struggle against the mode of distribution, instead of basing it on a struggle against the mode of production, the conception of class antagonism as an antagonism between the poor and the rich, the effort to graft the "co-operative principle" on capitalist economy all the nice notions found in Bernstein's doctrine already existed before him. And these theories were, in their time, in spite of their insufficiency, effective theories of the proletarian class struggle. They were the children's seven-league boots thanks to which the proletariat learned to walk upon the scene of history.

But after the development of the class struggle and its reflex in its social conditions had led to the abandonment of these theories and to the elaboration of the principles of scientific socialism, there could be no socialism at least in Germany outside of Marxist socialism and there could be no socialist class struggle outside of the Social-Democracy. From then on, socialism and Marxism, the proletarian struggle for emancipation and the Social-Democracy, were identical. That is why the return to pre-Marxist socialist theories no longer signifies today a return to the seven-league boots of the childhood of the proletariat, but a return to the puny worn-out slippers of the bourgeoisie.

Bernstein's theory was the first, and at the same time, the last attempt to give a theoretic base to opportunism. It is the last, because in Bernstein's system, opportunism has gone negatively through its renunciation of scientific socialism, positively through its marshalling of every bit of theoretic confusion possible as far as it can. In Bernstein's book, opportunism has crowned its theoretic development (just as it completed its practical development in the position taken by Schippel on the question of militarism) and has reached its ultimate conclusion.

Marxist doctrine can not only refute opportunism theoretically. It alone can explain opportunism as an historic phenomenon in the development of the party. The forward march of the proletariat, on a world historic scale, to its final victory is not, indeed, "so simple a thing." The peculiar character of this movement resides precisely in the fact that here, for the first time in history, the popular masses themselves, in opposition to the ruling classes, are to impose their will but they must affect this outside of the present society, beyond the existing society. This will the masses can only form in a constant struggle against the existing order. The union of the broad popular masses with an aim reaching beyond the existing social order, the union of the daily struggle with the great world transformation, that is the task of the Social-Democratic movement, which must logically grope on its road of development between the following two rocks, abandoning the mass character of the party or abandoning its final aim falling into bourgeois reformism or into sectarianism, anarchism, or opportunism.

In its theoretic arsenal, Marxist doctrine furnished, more than half a century ago, arms that are effective against both of these two extremes. But because our movement is a mass movement and because the dangers menacing it are not derived from the human brain but from social conditions, Marxist doctrine could not assure us, in advance and once for always, against the anarchist and opportunist tendencies. The latter can be overcome only as we pass from the domain of theory to the domain of practice but only with the help of the arms furnished us by Marx.

"Bourgeois revolutions," wrote Marx a half century ago, "like those of the eighteenth century, rush onward rapidly from success to success, their stage effects outbid one another, men and things seems to be set in flaming brilliants, ecstasy is the prevailing spirit; but they are short-lived, they reach their climax speedily and then society relapses into a long fit of nervous reaction before it learns how to appropriate the fruits of its period of feverish excitement. Proletarian revolutions, on the contrary, such as those of the nineteenth century, criticize themselves constantly; constantly interrupt themselves in their own course; come back to what seems to have been accomplished, in order to start anew; scorn with cruel thoroughness the half-measures, weakness and meanness of their first attempts; seem to throw down their adversary only to enable him to draw fresh strength from the earth and again to rise up against them in more gigantic stature; constantly recoil in fear before the undefined monster magnitude of their own objects until finally that situation is created which renders all retreats impossible and conditions themselves cry out: 'Hic Rhodus, hic salta!' Here is the rose. And here we must dance!" [Eighteenth Brumaire]

This has remained true even after the elaboration of the doctrine of scientific socialism. The proletarian movement has not as yet, all at once, become social-democratic, even in Germany. But it is becoming more social-democratic, surmounting continuously the extreme deviations of anarchism and opportunism, both of which are only determining phases of the development of the Social-Democracy, considered as a process.

For these reasons, we must say that the surprising thing here is not the appearance of an opportunist current but rather its feebleness.

As long as it showed itself in isolated cases of the practical activity of the party, one could suppose that it had a serious political base. But now that it has shown its face in Bernstein's book, one cannot help exclaiming with astonishment: "What? Is that all you have to say?" Not the shadow of an original thought! Not a single idea that was not refuted, crushed, reduced into dust by Marxism several decades ago!

It was enough for opportunism to speak out to prove it had nothing to say. In the history of our party that is the only importance of Bernstein's book.

Thus, saying good-bye to the mode of thought of the revolutionary proletariat, to dialectics and to the materialist conception of history, Bernstein can thank them for the attenuating circumstances they provide for his conversion. For only dialectics and the materialist conception of history, magnanimous as they are, could make Bernstein appear as an unconscious predestined instrument, by means of which the rising working class expresses its momentary weakness but which, upon closer inspection, it throws aside contemptuously and with pride.

– – –

LIST OF TITLES WITH ISBN NO.

ISBN	TITLE
9788194914129	1984
9789390575220	1984 & Animal Farm (2In1)
9789390575572	1984 & Animal Farm (2In1): The International Best-Selling Classics
9789390575848	35 Sonnets
9789390575329	A Clergyman's Daughter
9789390575923	A Study In Scarlet
9789390896097	A Tale Of Two Cities
9789390896837	Abide in Christ
9789390896202	Abraham Lincoln
9789390896912	Absolute Surrender
9789390896608	African American Classic Collection
9789390575305	Aldous Huxley: The Collected Works
9789390896141	An Autobiography of M. K. Gandhi
9789390575886	Animal Farm
9789390575619	Animal Farm & The Great Gatsby (2In1)
9789390575626	Animal Farm & We
9789390896158	Anna Karenina
9789390575534	Antic Hay
9789390896165	Antony & Cleopatra
9789390896172	As I Lay Dying
9789390896226	As You like it
9789390575671	At Your Command
9789390575350	Awakened Imagination
9789390575114	Be What You Wish
9789390896233	Believe In yourself
9789390896998	Best of Charles Darwin: The Origin of Species & Autobiography
9789390896684	Best Of Horror : Dracula And Frankenstein
9789390575503	Best Of Mark Twain (The Adventures of Tom Sawyer AND The Adventures of Huckleberry Finn)
9789390896769	Black History Collection
9789390575756	Brave New World, Animal Farm & 1984 (3in1)

9789390896240	Brother Karamzov
9789390575053	Bulleh Shah Poetry
9789390575725	Burmese Days
9789390896257	Bushido
9789390896066	Can't Hurt Me
9788194914112	Chanakya Neeti: With The Complete Sutras
9789390896042	Crime and Punishment
9789390575527	Crome Yellow
9789390575046	Down and Out in Paris and London
9789390896844	Dracula
9789390575442	Emersons Essays: The Complete First & Second Series (Self-Reliance & Other Essays)
9789390575749	Emma
9789390575817	Essential Tozer Collection - The Pursuit of God & The Purpose of Man
9789390896578	Fascism What It Is and How to Fight It
9789390575688	Feeling is the Secret
9789390575190	Five Lessons
9789390575954	Frankenstein
9789390575237	Franz Kafka: Collected Works
9789390575282	Franz Kafka: Short Stories
9789390575060	George Orwell Collected Works
9789390575077	George Orwell Essays
9789390575213	George Orwell Poems
9788194914150	Greatest Poetry Ever Written Vol 1
9788194914143	Greatest Poetry Ever Written Vol 1
9789390896301	Gulliver's Travel
9789390575961	Gunaho Ka Devta
9789390575893	H. P. Lovecraft Selected Stories Vol 1
9789390575978	H. P. Lovecraft Selected Stories Vol 2
9789390896059	Hamlet
9789390575022	His Last Bow: Some Reminiscences of Sherlock Holmes
9789390896134	History of Western Philosophy
9789390575121	Homage To Catalonia

9789390896219	How to develop self-confidence and Improve public Speaking
9789390896295	How to enjoy your life and your Job
9789390575633	How to own your own mind
9789390896318	How to read Human Nature
9789390896325	How to sell your way through the life
9789390896370	How to use the laws of mind
9789390896387	How to use the power of prayer
9789390896028	How to win friends & Influence People
9788194824176	How To Win Friends and Influence People
9789390896103	Humility The Beauty of Holiness
9789390896653	Imperialism the Highest Stage of Capitalism
9789390575084	In Our Time
9789390575169	In Our Time & Three Stories and Ten poems
9789390575145	James Allen: The Collected Works
9789390896189	Jesus Himself
9789390575480	Jo's Boys
9789390896394	Julius Caesar
9789390575404	Keep the Aspidistra Flying
9789390896400	Kidnapped
9789390896424	King Lear
9789390575824	Lady Susan
9789390896455	Law of Success
9789390896264	Lincoln The Unknown
9789390575565	Little Men
9789390575640	Little Women
9788194914174	Lost Horizon
9789390896462	Macbeth
9789390896929	Man Eaters of Kumaon
9789390896523	Man The Dwelling Place of God
9789390896349	Man The Dwelling Place of God
9789390575909	Mansfield Park
9788194914136	Manto Ki 25 Sarvshreshth Kahaniya
9789390896509	Marxism, Anarchism, Communism
9789390575664	Mathematical Principles of Natural Philosophy

9788194914198	Meditations
9789390575800	Mein Kampf
9789390575794	Memory How To Develop, Train, And Use It
9789390896486	Mind Power
9789390896585	Money
9789390575039	Mortal Coils
9789390575770	My Life and Work
9789390896035	Narrative of the Life of Frederick Douglass
9789390575152	Neville Goddard: The Collected Works
9789390575985	Northanger Abbey
9789390896530	Notes From Underground
9789390896547	Oliver Twist
9789390575459	On War
9789390575541	One, None and a Hundred Thousand
9789390896554	Othelo
9789390575435	Out Of This World
9789390575015	Persuasion
9789390575510	Prayer The Art Of Believing
9789390575091	Pride and Prejudice
9789390896561	Psychic Perception
9789390575381	Rabindranath Tagore - 5 Best Short Stories Vol 2
9789390575367	Rabindranath Tagore - Short Stories (Masters Collections Including The Childs Return)
9789390575374	Rabindranath Tagore 5 Best Short Stories Vol 1 (Including The Childs Return
9789390896622	Romeo & Juliet
9789390896127	Sanatana Dharma
9789390575596	Seedtime & Harvest
9789390896639	Selected Stories of Guy De Maupassant
9789390575206	Self-Reliance & Other Essays
9789390575176	Sense and Sensibility
9789390575299	Shyamchi Aai
9789390896738	Socialism Utopian and Scientific
9789390896646	Success Through a Positive Mental Attitude
9789390575428	The Adventures of Huckleberry Finn

9789390575183	The Adventures of Sherlock Holmes
9789390575343	The Adventures of Tom Sawyer
9789390896691	The Alchemy Of Happiness
9789390575862	The Art Of Public Speaking
9789390896288	The Autobiography Of Charles Darwin
9788194914181	The Best of Franz Kafka: The Metamorphosis & The Trial
9789390575008	The Call Of Cthulhu and Other Weird Tales
9789390575107	The Case-Book of Sherlock Holmes
9789390896110	The Castle Of Otranto
9789390896745	The Communist Manifesto
9789390575589	The Complete Fiction of H. P. Lovecraft
9789390575497	The Complete Works of Florence Scovel Shinn
9789390896820	The Conquest of Breard
9789390896813	The Diary of a Young Girl
9789390896332	The Diary of a Young Girl The Definitive Edition of the Worlds Most Famous Diary
9789390575701	The Great Gatsby, Animal Farm & 1984 (3In1)
9789390575312	The Greatest Works Of George Orwell (5 Books) Including 1984 & Non-Fiction
9789390575992	The Hound of Baskervilles
9789390896707	The Idiot
9789390896714	The Invisible Man
9789390575657	The Knowledge of the holy
9789390575558	The Law & the Promise
9789390896721	The Law Of Attraction
9789390896776	The Leader in you
9789390896363	The Life of Christ
9789390896196	The Man-Eating Leopard of Rudraprayag
9789390896783	The Master Key to Riches
9789390575268	The Memoirs Of Sherlock Holmes
9789390896479	The Midsummer Night's Dream
9789390575466	The Mill On The Floss
9789390896790	The Miracles of your mind
9789390896660	The Mutual Aid A Factor in Evolution
9789390896448	The Origin of Species

9789390896905	The Peter Kropotkin Anthology The Conquest of Bread & Mutual Aid A Factor of Evolution
9789390896806	The Picture of Dorian Gray
9789390896271	The Picture of Dorian Gray
9789390575275	The Power Of Awareness
9789390896356	The Power of Concentration
9788194824169	The Power of Positive Thinking
9789390575411	The Power of the Spoken Word
9788194914105	The Power Of Your Subconscious Mind
9789390896899	The Power of Your Subconscious Mind
9789390896417	The Principles of Communism
9789390575787	The Psychology Of Mans Possible Evolution
9789390896615	The Psychology of Salesmanship
9789390575732	The Pursuit of God
9789390575398	The Pursuit of Happiness
9789390896851	The Quick and Easy Way to effective Speaking
9789390575947	The Return Of Sherlock Holmes
9789390575138	The Road To Wigan Pier
9789390896981	The Root of the Righteous
9789390575855	The Science Of Being Well
9788194914167	The Science Of Getting Rich, The Science Of Being Great & The Science Of Being Well (3In1)
9789390896011	The Screwtape Letters
9789390896073	The Screwtape Letters
9789390575336	The Secret Door to Success
9789390575695	The Secret Of Imagining
9789390896868	The Secret Of Success
9789390896431	The Seven Last Words
9789390575930	The Sign of the Four
9789390896004	The Sonnets
9789390896516	The Souls of Black Folk
9789390896875	The Sound and The Fury
9789390575244	The State and Revolution
9789390896882	The Story of My Life
9789390896936	The Story Of Oriental Philosophy

9789390896752	The Strange Case of Dr. Jekyll and Mr. Hyde
9789390896943	The Tempest
9789390575916	The Valley Of Fear
9789390575879	The Wind in the willows
9789390896080	The Wind in the willows
9789390575763	Their eyes were watching gofd
9789390575831	Three Stories
9789390896950	Twelfth Night
9789390896592	Twelve Years a Slave
9789390896677	Up from Slavery
9789390896974	Value Price and Profit
9789390896967	Wake Up and Live
9789390896493	With Christ in the School of Prayer
9789390575602	Your Faith is Your Fortune
9789390575473	Your Infinite Power To Be Rich
9789390575251	Your Word is Your Wand
9789390575718	Youth
9789391316099	A Christmas Carol
9789391316105	A Doll's House
9789391316501	A Passage to India
9789391316709	A Portrait of the Artist as a Young Man
9789391316112	A Tale of Two Cities
9789391316747	A Tear and a Smile
9789391316167	Agnes Gray
9789391316174	Alice's Adventures in Wonderland
9789391316136	Anandamath
9789391316181	Anne Of Green Gables
9789391316754	Anthem
9789391316198	Around The World in 80 Days
9789391316013	As A Man Thinketh
9789391316242	Autobiography of a Yogi
9789391316266	Beyond Good and Evil
9789391316761	Bleak House
9789391316778	Chitra, a Play in One Act
9789391316310	David Copperfield

9789391316075	Demian
9789391316785	Dubliners
9789391316051	Favourite Tales from the Arabian Nights
9789391316235	Gitanjali
9789391316068	Gravity
9789391316150	Great Speeches of Abraham Lincoln
9789391316662	Guerilla Warfare
9789391316839	Kim
9789391316822	Mother
9789391316211	My Childhood
9789391316846	Nationalism
9789391316327	Oliver Twist
9789391316853	Pygmalion
9789391316334	Relativity: The Special and the General Theory
9789391316389	Scientific Healing Affirmation
9789391316341	Sons and Lovers
9789391316587	Tales from India
9789391316372	Tess of The D'Urbervilles
9789391316396	The Awakening and Selected Stories
9789391316402	The Bhagvad Gita
9789391316303	The Book of Enoch
9789391316228	The Canterville Ghost
9789391316907	The Dynamic Laws of Prosperity
9789391316006	The Great Gatsby
9789391316860	The Hungry Stones and Other Stories
9789391316433	The Idiot
9789391316440	The Importance of Being Earnest
9789391316297	The Light of Asia
9789391316914	The Madman His Parables and Poems
9789391316457	The Odyssey
9789391316921	The Picture of Dorian Gray
9789391316464	The Prince
9789391316938	The Prophet
9789391316945	The Republic
9789391316518	The Scarlet Letter

9789391316143	The Seven Laws of Teaching
9789391316525	The Story of My Experiments with Truth
9789391316532	The Tales of the Mother Goose
9789391316549	The Thirty Nine Steps
9789391316594	The Time Machine
9789391316600	The Turn of the Screw
9789391316983	The Upanishads
9789391316617	The Yellow Wallpaper
9789391316426	The Yoga Sutras of Patanjali
9789391316990	Ulysses
9789391316624	Utopia
9789391316679	Vanity Fair
9789391316020	What Is To Be Done
9789391316686	Within A Budding Grove
9789391316693	Women in Love

www.ingramcontent.com/pod-product-compliance
Ingram Content Group UK Ltd.
Pitfield, Milton Keynes, MK11 3LW, UK
UKHW040318300826
14791UKWH00003B/966